HISTORIC PENNSYLVANIA

An Illustrated History

By William A. Pencak

Commissioned by the Pennsylvania Chamber of Business and Industry

Historical Publishing Network
A division of Lammert Incorporated
San Antonio, Texas

FOR VINCENT ANDRASSY, TEXAN BY BIRTH, PENNSYLVANIAN BY CHOICE.

CONTENTS

ISBN: 9781893619883
Library of Congress Card Catalog Number: 2008932343

Historic Pennsylvania: An Illustrated History
author: Willaim A. Pencak
contributing writers for "Sharing the Heritage":
Eric Dabney, Joe Goodpasture, Scott Williams

Historical Publishing Network
president: Ron Lammert
project managers: Joe & Robin Neely, Roger Smith
administration: Donna M. Mata, Melissa Quinn
book sales: Dee Steidle
production: Colin Hart, Craig Mitchell, Chuck Newton, Evelyn Hart, Roy Arellano

SPECIAL THANKS

- Professor Russell Graham, curator of the Edward Steidle Museum of the College of Earth and Mineral Science, Penn State University. A few of the museum's paintings may be seen in the Deike Building on the Penn State campus, and more on the museum website. Unfortunately, there is limited space to display most of the approximately five hundred images, the finest collection of industrial paintings in the world.
- Beverly Balger Sutley, registrar of the Palmer Museum of Art, Penn State University. Over three hundred images of the O'Connor/Yeager Collection of American prints, donated by former owners of the Tavern Restaurant in State College (which still displays an extensive collection on its walls) are available online at the Penn State website.
- Sandra Stelts, Special Collections Librarian Pattee/Paterno Libraries, Penn State University. The entire Ammon-Stapleton Collection of fraktur may also be viewed online at the Penn State Libraries website.
- Graciella Marchietti, curator of the Southern Alleghenies Museum of Art, Loreto, Pennsylvania. The Museum's fine collections at four sites: Loreto, Ligonier, Johnstown, and Altoona, may be viewed on its website.
- Brenda Wetzel, the Pennsylvania Historical and Museum Commission.
- Michael Sherbon and Linda Ries, the Pennsylvania State Archives.
- Nathan Houser, the Charles Peirce Papers, Indiana University-Purdue University, Indianapolis.
- The Yuengling Brewery.
- Mack Trucks.
- The Mifflinburg Buggy Museum.
- The staff of the Thomas T. Taber Museum of Art, the Lycoming County Historical Society, Williamsport, Pennsylvania.
- The Prints and Photographs Online Collection of the Library of Congress.
- Special Collections, Van Pelt Library, the University of Pennsylvania (the photographs from the Marian Anderson Collection may be viewed online).
- The Philadelphia Mural Arts Commission, which has sponsored several hundred murals that enliven the city and is interested in sponsoring more. These may be viewed online (including several murals which have been demolished – http://www.muralarts.org).
- Randall Miller and Peter Potter, who taught me how to choose images.

FOR FURTHER READING

Randall Miller and William Pencak, *Pennsylvania: A History of the Commonwealth* (Penn State Press, 2002). The only extensive history of the state now in print, with over five hundred illustrations, maps, and charts. Chronological chapters and chapters on how to use geography, archaeology, painting, folklore, literature, genealogy, photography, architecture, and oral history interviews to understand the state's history.

Journals

Pennsylvania History, c/o Karen Guenther, History Department, Mansfield University, Mansfield, PA.

The Pennsylvania Magazine of History and Biography, The Historical Society of Pennsylvania, 1300 Locust St., Philadelphia, PA, 19107.

Pennsylvania Heritage, The Pennsylvania Heritage Society, 400 North St., Harrisburg, PA 17120.

Western Pennsylvania History, The Historical Society of Western Pennsylvania, 1212 Smallwood St., Pittsburgh, PA, 15222.

Several counties, including Berks, Lancaster, Centre, and Lycoming have excellent historical journals.

Websites

http://www.libraries.psu.edu/artshumanities/history/pahistory.htm—a link to numerous websites that provide information on the state's history, maintained by the Arts and Humanities Library at Penn State University.

http://www.explorepahistory.com—uses the state's historical markers as the basis for wide-ranging discussions of the state's history. Includes many illustrations and documents.

PENNSYLVANIA'S UNIQUE HISTORY

"We have such a rich history, second to no other state, and we make little use of it in developing pride in our state." So wrote Governor George Leader, whose own achievements in promoting
the state's economy, welfare, and system of education form an important part of that history, fifty
years after he took office in 1955. Pennsylvania is one of four states (Massachusetts, Virginia, and
Kentucky are the others) to call itself a Commonwealth and used to announced that motorists
entering the state with signs that "AMERICA STARTS HERE." But it no longer does. Perhaps other
states objected. Auto license plates used to carry the state's motto, "THE KEYSTONE STATE," but
now simply display the state flag's principal colors (blue, white, and yellow) and a website where
people can learn about Pennsylvania (state.pa.us).

These signs and license plates are important, and each conveys an important truth. Many of the
ideas and practices America introduced to modern the world began in Pennsylvania. Yes, people of
Massachusetts can talk about how the Pilgrims and Puritans arrived over fifty years before William

Penn founded Pennsylvania in 1682, and how they too came seeking religious freedom, as did the Pennsylvania Quakers. But the freedom they sought for themselves they denied to others; Pennsylvania offered any peaceable citizen the right to worship as he or she pleased. New York also contained an impressive mixture of people of different nationalities when it was founded as New Amsterdam in 1624. But New York fought repeatedly with the Indians, and the people physically fought fiercely among themselves and with their rulers. They were so divided that when the English took over in 1664, for once, the soon-to-be New Yorkers did not live up to their feisty reputation. They defied the orders of their unpopular, one-legged governor, Peter Stuyvesant, and refused to fight the enemy. Pennsylvanians, on the other hand, although they did not always agree about everything, maintained their society for seventy-five years without either a rebellion or any military force whatsoever.

Other people who started earlier made even less of an impression. The Norsemen, who arrived around the year 1000, and the Spanish, who established St. Augustine in Florida in 1565, both have a claim to previous settlements, but those of the Norse did not last, and no continuous stream of settlement followed. St. Augustine is the oldest continuously occupied city in the territory that became the United States, but for the first two hundred years of its history it was basically a small Spanish military

outpost in Florida. As for Jamestown, established in 1607, it ceased to exist within a century: all that remains are archaeological ruins of Virginia's first capital, a colony where after twenty years, only 1,000 of 6,000 immigrants survived.

Of course, the first Americans were really the people we call Indians or Native Americans. Here Pennsylvania does have a claim to be first in one way that has not yet been challenged, although a future discovery might change things. The oldest archaeological site in the Western Hemisphere where human remains have been found is Meadowcroft in Washington County, Pennsylvania, in the extreme southwestern corner of the state. Scientists have dated it to 14,000 to 16,000 years ago using carbon testing—the element carbon decays at a known rate and can be found in all buried materials. To be sure, people must have lived elsewhere in the hemisphere before they arrived in what became Pennsylvania. There just is no hard evidence at the time this book was written.

"Keystone State" comes from an architect's term. The stone at the top of an arch, necessary to complete it and keep it from falling, is known as the keystone. Pennsylvania was called "the keystone in the democratic arch," the large state in the middle of the original thirteen, whose support was necessary to ensure the success of the American Revolution and the new American nation.

VISIT PENNSYLVANIA

WHERE PRE·REVOLUTIONARY COSTUMES STILL SURVIVE

But Pennsylvania is more than that. For each of the last four centuries, Pennsylvania—yes, America as a whole but very specifically Pennsylvania—led the human race into the world we have today. For instance, in the 1600s, the world marveled at the idea that people of different religions and ethnic groups could coexist under the same government without slaughtering each other. Even in 2005, outside of Europe and the United States, such tolerance is hard to find. Yet Pennsylvania and its visionary founder William Penn implemented these ideas from the very first. In the 1700s, the world marveled again—at the fact that a similarly diverse people could establish a large, independent nation that did not require a standing army or aristocracy to keep them in line.

(Again, even today, in how many nations do we see soldiers patrolling the streets?) Pennsylvania was the "keystone" to the success of the Revolution and the new nation. The Declaration of Independence and the United States Constitution saw the light of day in Philadelphia, where ethnically diverse statesmen with different religious beliefs from the entire nation proved they could agree on a government much as the people of Pennsylvania had originally done. And could we imagine a Revolution without Benjamin Franklin, whose rise from poverty to world fame as the first authentic American genius was the mirror image of the nation itself?

In the 1800s, Pennsylvania was a keystone of a different sort—one that enabled the United States to become the world's greatest economic power (outpacing Britain by around 1850), a position it still holds. New York, to be sure, had more people and generated greater wealth. But New York's wealth was commercial rather than industrial; it was based on shipping, the southern cotton trade, importing goods from around the world, and select industries such as publishing and making clothes that could be done within the small confines of Manhattan Island. Pennsylvania produced much, if not most, of the coal, iron, steel, lumber, and (until the Texas boom after 1900) oil in the United States. Given its mountainous terrain, it also led the nation in transportation: roads, canals, and railroads linked the corners of the state to each other and then to the markets of the west and south. In 1900, the largest corporation in the world was the Pennsylvania Railroad, and, when US Steel took over that honor the following year, most of its wealth came from Pennsylvania. A list of Pennsylvania industrial "firsts" goes on and on: the first US bank, the first steamboat, the first insurance company, the first paved road that went beyond city limits—the original "Pennsylvania Turnpike," which connected Lancaster and Philadelphia by 1794—the first building lighted by electricity (in Sunbury), and so on. Nor should we forget that Pennsylvania's working people led in the struggles to form unions and ensure better working conditions. The Franklin Typographers of Philadelphia went on the first strike in America (in 1786), the Knights of Labor flourished first in Scranton and were led by Scranton's mayor Terence Powderly, the American Federation of Labor (AFL) and the Congress of Industrial Organizations (CIO) were founded in Pittsburgh.

For the 1900s, the picture is less rosy. Pennsylvania still pioneered in important ways. The University of Pennsylvania put the world's first computer into operation in 1946, a huge contraption the size of a football field that any hand-held computer can outperform today. Pennsylvania also leads the nation in the production of nuclear energy. Here, of course, the troubles begin. Think nuclear energy and "Three Mile Island" comes to mind, the plant near Middletown, Pennsylvania where in 1979 a reactor malfunction almost led to a catastrophe. Yet it didn't, and scientific studies show that there is no evidence anyone was killed or harmed, unlike Chernobyl. As the price of oil rises, nuclear power (extensively used in Europe) may prove Pennsylvania right. The state still has plenty of coal and a huge natural gas deposit discovered in 2008.

But the main trend of late twentieth century Pennsylvania has been deindustrialization: the decline of big industry. Steel towns and coal towns where the factories and mines have closed have become symbols of the state, as movies such as *The Deer Hunter* or *All the Right Moves* indicate. Available coal, oil, and forests ran out (nearly every tree in Pennsylvania is less that a 150 years old), and Pennsylvania workers, proud of their tradition of organized labor, would not work under conditions that prevail in the Third World. While not actually declining, Pennsylvania's population has risen much slower than the national average since 1960. The second largest state in the union from 1820 until 1970, it now trails not only New York but California, Florida, and Texas. Philadelphia, the third largest city in the nation for most of the twentieth century, has lost a quarter of its population since 1970, and Pittsburgh nearly a half.

So do we conclude on a sad note? Not necessarily. In the historical long run, nothing lasts forever, and it was logical that as Pennsylvania led the American industrial revolution, as the world economy changed and resources are not infinite, it would also lead in experiencing the decline of that traditional industrial economy. The invention of the computer at the University of Pennsylvania was a sign of things to come. Pennsylvania is now adjusting to the service economy in which the United States now leads the world. For instance, Pittsburgh and Philadelphia are world-class medical care and research centers rather than industrial ones. As center cities' populations go down, those of the surrounding areas rise.

But there is something more. Pennsylvania has its history, its incredibly diverse history. People come from around the world to visit Independence Hall and downtown Philadelphia. But they can also observe the Amish in Lancaster and Centre Counties and the Moravians in Bethlehem, not as portrayed by reenactors, but still farming fields that after two or three centuries constitute some of the richest agricultural land on the planet. Travelers through the state encounter an astonishing number of historical sites and museums—maintained by the state, federal, and local governments as well as private associations—that honor scientists (Joseph Priestley, who discovered oxygen), coal miners (Eckley Miners Village), farmers (the Landis Valley Farm Museum), African Americans (the African American Museum in Philadelphia), and industrialists (the Frick mansion in Pittsburgh, the Asa Packer in Jim Thorpe.) There are also the beautiful forests and rivers maintained by the state and houses in old towns lovingly restored by their owners. Not only the State Museum in Harrisburg, but the incredible artwork in the adjoining State Capitol are testaments to this history.

History is now a big industry in Pennsylvania. The two most frequently seen "vanity" auto license plates not only depict the Pennsylvania railroad and the battleship *Niagara* (that won the naval battle in Lake Erie during the War of 1812) but the revenue from their sale promotes the state's history programs. People who care about history, who like to explore old communities, who seek woodland beauty, and who want to think about where our nation came from, what troubles it has endured, and what are its possible futures could do no better than to live in, travel throughout, or study Pennsylvania.

NATIVE AMERICANS

Several years ago, Indians in eastern Pennsylvania objected that the name of Delaware Avenue, the first street in Philadelphia that runs parallel to the Delaware River, was changed to Columbus Boulevard. Ironically, they were defending the name the Leni Lenape Indians in the region received from Europeans, who named the river after Lord De la Warr, an early English governor of Virginia. But they had made the word "Delaware" their own, and the words we choose to describe historical events and people in history tell us a great deal about how we value them.

For instance, it is customary to describe the "settlement" of America. Settling conveys the idea of a comfortable, pleasant process. In South America, the occupation of the continent by Europeans is called the "conquest," a name that would accurately describe what happened almost everywhere—with Pennsylvania being the greatest exception in America both North and South. We call the first white people to enter a region its pioneers, that is, forward thinking people, idealists of vision and courage. The Spanish called them *conquistadores*—those who conquered.

Indian groups, or societies, or nations, or peoples are sometimes called "tribes," a word that in English has a negative meaning: a group of people who live in a primitive way with little change and progress. But Native American societies were in motion centuries before the Europeans came, forming and reforming societies, a process that the white "invasion"—to use another word sometimes substituted for settlement—accelerated. Similarly, historians now prefer the word "encounter" to "discovery": if Europeans first set eyes on new peoples, so did Indians, as each group learned from and absorbed customs and ideas from the other. Indians were not, in short, passive victims of Europeans.

The term Indian is sometimes disputed as well, since of course Columbus did not encounter the people of that name in Asia as he thought. But "Native Americans" usually accept "Indian" as a sensible alternative, since it does not put them down as does "redskin" or "savage" (Native American can be confusing, too, since it can also mean anybody born in America.) The idea that Indians are "red," however, is not only false, as anyone who has ever met an Indian will note, but only came into general use in the era of the American Revolution. By designating all Indians as "red," and possessing certain innate characteristics—warlike, uncivilized, savage—white Americans could claim that they were all unchangeably

inferior, worthy only to be removed or exterminated if they failed to leave territory the whites desired. They became a distinctive "race" at this time. But for most of the colonial period, until the American Revolution, a "middle ground" stretching from the Delaware, Mohawk, and Susquehanna Valleys to the western Ohio, existed where whites and Indians interacted and lived side-by-side, not always in harmony, but respecting each other, making alliances or engaging in conflicts. Who was friends with whom—especially whether Indians were pro-English, pro-French, and later pro-American—was much more important than who was Indian or white.

What do we really know about the original people William Penn encountered in 1682 when he first landed in Philadelphia? The familiar image of Penn making "a" treaty with "the" Indians is a myth, largely fostered by Benjamin West's famous 1772 painting. Actually, West's painting was ordered by Penn's grandson, then the proprietor of Pennsylvania, who at the time was fighting to retain his rule against Pennsylvanians represented in Britain by Benjamin Franklin. They were hoping to turn it into a colony governed by the king and proprietor John Penn wanted to point out that it was his ancestor who had maintained peace with the natives and given this prosperous colony to Britain. But in fact, since the Philadelphia region contained several small but independent groups of Indians, Penn had to make several treaties.

Furthermore, the Indians only thought they were giving the whites the right to use land they actually farmed. Otherwise they hoped to share it, rather than agreeing to leave the territory forever. As larger number of settlers than they had ever seen arrived quickly, they were forced to move west not by force, but simply because they no longer had lands on which to hunt. Hence, the Delaware, Shawnee, and Munsee, three of the main groups of Algonquin Indians who lived in eastern Pennsylvania when Penn arrived, were living in the Midwest—Kentucky, Ohio, and southern Michigan—by the 1750s. West of these three peoples initially dwelled the Susquehannocks in the river valley that bears their name, and west of them we know little.

Whites and Indians rarely understood each other, despite valiant efforts by intermediaries on both sides such as Madame Montour, a part

French-Canadian, part-Indian woman for whom the state's Montour County is named, and Conrad Weiser who lived just west of Reading. For the whites, nature and all creation were given by God to human beings to use for their benefit; for the Indians, animals, plants, rivers, and mountains were spiritual equals in a universe that had to be used cautiously and preserved for future generations, as nineteenth-century conservationists, notably Pennsylvania's Gifford Pinchot, began to tell us. Whites looked at Indian women as exploited "squaws," since they did the farmwork and housework while the men went off hunting. In Europe, hunting was a recreation reserved for the wealthy that in America became universal among men. For the Indians, it was work that required following game for long periods and bringing back sufficient quantities to feed a village

✧

Even before William Penn landed in 1682, European trade goods had reached the interior of what is now Pennsylvania, as archaeological remains show. The Susquehannock Indians were able to carve more sophisticated combs thanks to European items. A rum bottle, spoon, snuffbox, glass beads, Swedish ceramic bowl, metal kettles, flintlock musket mechanism, metal harpoon, cut Delft ceramic dish, brass arrowheads, iron axes, a Jew's harp, and tobacco pipes were among the items found at archaeological sites. They were probably obtained indirectly from the Swedes in New Sweden, Dutch in New Netherland, or English in Maryland and Virginia.

COURTESY OF THE PENNSYLVANIA HISTORICAL AND MUSEUM COMMISSION.

for weeks or months. Nor could whites understand why when a council with the Indians occurred, several hundred people came, including large numbers of women with whom the men frequently talked. Women's opinions counted for much in Indian society, and even "nations" such as the Iroquois that were regarded by whites as "nations" were composed of small, independent groups who made their own decisions. As divorce was easy in Indian society, people traced their descent through their mother: one's father could be in doubt, but never one's mother. Indians raised their children without beating them, far more humanely than many whites in the seventeenth century. In many ways, with its respect for

women, children, and community decision-making, Indian society resembled our own more than the society of the white Europeans who replaced them. Whites who were taken captive by the Indians frequently wanted to remain; that was rarely true of Indians captured by whites.

Yet if European and Indian Pennsylvanians did not understand each other well, they nevertheless managed to live in peace from 1682 to 1755, and without any significant land swindles until 1737. Not only William Penn's children and grandchildren, but the Indians themselves a hundred years later, would fondly remember the days of "Onas," as they called William Penn, when the guns were silent and the knives were sheathed.

✧

William Penn's Treaty with the Indians, *John Boydell's 1775 print based on the 1772 painting by Benjamin West.*

COURTESY OF THE LIBRARY OF CONGRESS.

PENNSYLVANIA BEGINNINGS: WILLIAM PENN AND THE QUAKERS

Today, in the Philadelphia area, Quakers are known mostly as kindly people who run several excellent private schools, dress plainly and conservatively, and peacefully protest war, violence, and capital punishment. This was not originally the case. During the English Civil War (1640-1649) and the rule of Oliver Cromwell (1649-1658), the Society of Friends, as they called themselves, was one of dozens of religious groups that emerged from the chaos of the period. To the average Anglican; that is a member of the Church of England (later the Episcopal Church in America) or Presbyterian, the two leading religious groups in the nation, it mattered little whether some religious extremist was a Quaker, a Ranter, an Anabaptist, a Leveller, a Digger, or a Muggletonian—the last of these believing one Lodowick Muggleton was one of the two witnesses mentioned in the Book of Revelation. All were perceived as threats to both state and church, to order in society, and deserving to be eliminated.

But the Society of Friends—who adopted the name "Quaker" (it came from the way their bodies shook when the Holy Spirit moved them) and with which their enemies mocked them—was the only so-called religious extremist group to survive. At first they were as obnoxious as all the rest and could easily be confused with them. They would barge in on other churches' services, or disrupt them with noise in the streets. One early Quaker even rode into a city on Easter Sunday on the back of a donkey while his followers sang Hosannas, strongly implying they thought he was the Second Coming of Christ. But by the 1660s, the Quakers were behaving differently. Under the guidance of George Fox, they had adopted pacifism and the idea that no one could be converted to the true religion, which they still believed to be theirs and none other, except through persuasion and the "Inner Light" that dwelled in all human beings.

✧

The Landing of William Penn *by Jean L. G. Ferris, a nineteenth-century French artist.* COURTESY OF THE LIBRARY OF CONGRESS.

For Quakers, the equal presence of the Inner Light translated itself into religious equality within the church. There were no Quaker bishops or priests, although people who exhibited special holiness were honored and those who spoke to the unconverted were called preachers or, if they traveled, missionaries. Women as well as men could speak at Quaker meetings, where people simply gathered in a "Meeting House" (not a church) and waited until the Holy Spirit moved someone to speak. (If it did not, people just went home.) Quakers took the idea of human equality on a spiritual plane seriously: everyone addressed each other as "thee" or "thou," rather than "you." This familiar form has vanished from the English language although not in other western European languages (France has "tu" and "vous," German "du" and "sie," for instance.) Everyone was a "friend" rather than a "sir" or "my lord." Quakers had to wear plain clothes, grey or black in color, and could not take off their hats and bow to honor people of higher ranks. There is a story which, if it isn't true, should be: when William Penn met King Charles II in the royal palace, the king—who

was personally rather tolerant and of a humorous bent—took off his hat and bowed to Penn. "Friend Charles, why dost thou remove thy hat?" asked Penn. "Because," replied the king, "tis the custom of the palace, when two people meet, one removes his hat."

What, you may ask, was Penn doing in the palace? Most Quakers were poor people, to whom the idea of equality with the wealthy had an obvious appeal. But the faith also attracted wealthy women, for whom it promised equality and an active role, and men of means who were moved by the zealous Quaker preachers. William Penn, however, was in a class by himself. His father Admiral Sir William Penn was responsible for making sure that the royal navy supported King Charles II when he returned from exile in 1660. He also was the most successful English admiral before Lord Nelson, defeating the Dutch decisively in the two Anglo-Dutch Wars of the 1650s and 1660s that made England the world's greatest naval power, a position it held until World War II. Additionally, he lent the king a good deal of money and was his personal friend.

But he was not a good father. He was away at sea much of the time, and young William rebelled. First, he joined the army rather than the navy, and fought for English Protestants trying to conquer Ireland. Then he became a Quaker, the seventeenth-century equivalent of the child of an American admiral becoming a Communist. He served three terms in jail for preaching, refusing to let his father use his influence to free him. His second trial, which occurred in 1667, was an important landmark in the history of civil liberties: when the judges ordered the jury to convict him on the grounds that he was preaching to an unlawful assembly, they refused, and thereby established the fact that a jury did not have to accept a judge's interpretation of the law. His final imprisonment of six months only ended shortly before his father's death in 1670, when he was released to make his peace with the dying man.

Of all the Quakers, the twenty-six-year-old Penn was the wealthiest and certainly most prestigious. In the 1670s, he visited sympathetic people in Holland and German states in the Rhineland and interested himself in the settlement of West and East Jersey in the 1670s. But his dream was to found a Quaker colony, which in 1682 the king granted him in exchange for the debts he had inherited from his father. The king and his advisors were quite happy to put three thousand miles of ocean between themselves, the Quakers, and the sort of people Penn hoped would populate his colony. With a hint of irony, King Charles named the colony "Pennsylvania"—not after William Penn, but after the father with whom he had so frequently argued. Penn would have simply preferred "Sylvania"—or woodlands.

Penn had no trouble finding people willing to populate his colony. He offered almost free land not only to English Quakers, but to others who showed sympathy toward them and to pacifists from Germany who sought to escape persecution. The "almost" was the catch: Penn not only hoped to further God's work, but he wanted to make a profit on his colony by collecting quitrents—individually small but collectively a large sum—from those to whom he granted land. He also hoped to develop a substantial estate for himself, which has been reconstructed as a state historical

site at Pennsbury Manor just north of Philadelphia on the Delaware River.

Then there was the question of Pennsylvania's government. Having been educated at Oxford, Penn had read a great deal of political theory—and, with Thomas Hobbes, James Harrington, and John Locke, seventeenth century England was a great age of political theory. He initially proposed an elaborate constitution where officials of various sorts would comprise an enormous council (roughly equivalent to a senate) while the landowners would elect an even larger assembly. Objections to this plan, along with a dislike of the quitrents, forced Penn to change his mind—again and again. By the time Pennsylvania worked out its final, and extremely simple, constitution in 1701, 18 other plans had been proposed and either rejected or implemented briefly in 20 years. Ultimately, freeholders (those who owned a middle-sized plot of land or property in a town) elected an assembly; the proprietor appointed the governor (unless he chose to govern in person) and other officials such as sheriffs for each county and justices of the peace; laws had to be approved by both the

✧

Penn House—Originally believed to be built for William Penn in 1682, the house located at 3400 Girard Avenue in Fairmount Park was actually built around 1715 for Thomas Chalkley, a Philadelphia merchant and Quaker preacher, on land near 2nd and Chestnut Streets. In 1883, the city bought the building and moved it to Fairmount Park. It is located at the Philadelphia Zoo, where it served as an office building for years.

assembly and the proprietor or his deputy. Unlike the other British colonies, Pennsylvania had no upper house or council—appointed by the crown except in Rhode Island, Massachusetts, and Connecticut—that acted as an upper house to balance the assembly. The Pennsylvania councilors were simply prominent men who advised the governor or his deputy.

Penn, unfortunately, was not able to enjoy life in the colony that gave freedom and prosperity to so many settlers. He remained from 1682 to 1684, when he returned to England. There, he befriended the Catholic King James II (ruled 1685-1688), who offered him friendship and religious toleration before he was overthrown in the "Glorious Revolution" of 1688 for trying to rule without the consent of Parliament. Suspected as a traitor, Penn was briefly imprisoned. When released, he discovered that he was losing money on Pennsylvania, so much so that when he tried to sell it, no one wanted to buy. Only in 1699 did he return for two years and work out the constitution before he went back to England once more, this time to dispute with Lord Baltimore, the proprietor of Maryland, where Pennsylvania ended and Maryland began. (Only the Mason-Dixon line laid out in 1763 solved this problem.)

Penn suffered a serious stroke in 1708 that left him helpless for the final six years of his life. During that time, and until his sons were old enough to rule, his widow, Hannah Callowhill Penn, with the advice of James Logan, the able province secretary, ruled the province far more effectively than Penn himself had. By 1726, harmony was established between the governor and assembly that lasted until the French and Indian War broke out in 1755. Hannah Penn even turned a profit on quitrents and land sales.

Who lived in Penn's colony? When he first arrived, he was greeted by about five hundred Swedes and Finns who had already settled in the Delaware Valley. In the early 1600s, Sweden was one of the great military powers in Europe and wanted to join the Spanish, English, French, and Dutch in obtaining colonies. In 1637, the New Sweden Company hired Peter Minuit, who had founded the Dutch colony of New Amsterdam thirteen years earlier, to begin a settlement of its own. In 1638, Minuit began Fort Christina at what is now Wilmington, Delaware, but the colony did not flourish. In 1643, the company appointed a new governor, Johan Printz, to put the colony in order. Weighing about 400 pounds and nearly seven feet tall, Printz's personality was as imposing as his appearance. He moved the settlement northward to what is now Tinicum Island just south of Philadelphia, the first permanent white settlement in land that became Pennsylvania.

Despite Printz' best efforts, New Sweden remained tiny. Sweden usually sent one ship per year to the settlement; several were lost and one came with disease. The company hoped to turn a profit either growing tobacco, like Virginia to the south, or trading for furs with the Indians, like New Netherland to the north, but the settlers wanted to grow food and prosper for themselves rather than work for the company. The settlers disliked Printz's dictatorial ways; when they protested, he executed the leader. Discouraged at Sweden's lack of support, Printz left for home in 1653. In a show of independence, however, his daughter, Armengott, remained in the New World as proprietor of her own prosperous farm. Two years later, seven Dutch ships commanded by New Netherland's Governor Peter Stuyvesant sailed down the Delaware River and took over the colony. In 1664, the English assumed control when they in turn conquered New Netherland, but basically the small settlement of about five hundred people was left on its own until William Penn arrived in 1682.

Despite its tiny size, New Sweden left several legacies to America. The log cabin was brought to the New World by the Finnish settlers that the Swedes recruited to help populate the colony, and it became the standard habitation for the American frontier. New Sweden established the pattern of peaceful relations with the Indians that Pennsylvania continued. The first Lutheran churches in North America came from Sweden. And because they arrived first, Swedish descendants populated the mid-Atlantic region far out of proportion to their tiny numbers. Although few people know it, the name "Rambo" that Philadelphia-born movie star Sylvester Stallone chose as the hero of one of his films comes from an early Swedish settler.

The Welsh and English settlers Penn recruited left their mark on the region, too. Names tell the story of where they settled: Welsh settlements included Tredyffin, Bala Cynwyd, and North Wales in the Philadelphia suburbs. Chester and Bristol, the first two counties formed along with Philadelphia, were also heavily English. But the interior, at least until the Scots-Irish came in large numbers after 1740, belonged to the Pennsylvania Germans, one of the most fascinating and persistent groups to settle America.

THE PENNSYLVANIA GERMANS

✧

Left and following page, top: Pennsylvania Dutch, notably the Amish, who live primarily in Lancaster County or in central Pennsylvania in Centre, Snyder, and Union counties. In 1693, a Swiss bishop, Jacob Amman broke off from the Mennonites (founded in 1536 by Menno Simons). To this day, the "Old Order" Amish dress mostly in black, and will not use modern technology such as cars and electricity. The Supreme Court ruled in 1972 that they were exempt on religious grounds from laws requiring public school attendance for their children. The "New Order" Amish are divided into various groups, some of whom receive more education and can use cars, electricity, etc. All are pacifists and live in distinct communities. In the 1960s, upset by the development in Lancaster County, many moved to central Pennsylvania to better retain their ways.

COURTESY OF THE AUTHOR.

Amish, Mennonites (or Church of the Brethren), Moravians, Dunkards (not Drunkards, I tell my students), Schwenkfelders, the Ephrata and Harmony societies. All of these pacifist groups came to Pennsylvania by the end of the colonial era to live in peace with their neighbors. Although the last four have disappeared, the Amish, Mennonites, and Moravians, after three hundred years, for the most part still flourish in Pennsylvania. Yet we need to remember that despite the fascinating histories of these groups, the overwhelming majority of the Pennsylvania Germans, at least 95 percent, were not pacifists and belonged to the mainstream Lutheran and Reformed (Calvinist) Churches. Collectively, they all became known as Pennsylvania "Dutch," not because they came from Holland, but because "deutsch," the German word for German, sounded like "Dutch" to the English. At the time of the American Revolution, they numbered about a third of Pennsylvania's some three hundred thousand people. Another 100,000 were Scots-Irish, and about a third English, making Pennsylvania the only one of the 13 colonies without an ethnically English majority.

✧

Below: Conrad Beissel, a charismatic leader who was head Elder of the Conestoga Congregation of the Brethren, established his own community at the Ephrata Cloisters in 1732. Unlike most Brethren, he stressed living an extremely ascetic life including renunciation of sexual intercourse, wearing coarse, simple clothing, and sleeping on narrow wooden boards. When he died in 1768, the community gradually died out. In 1941, the Pennsylvania Historical and Museum Commission took over the surviving structures, which are now a museum village.

COURTESY OF THE AUTHOR.

The appropriately named Germantown, originally about twelve miles northwest of Philadelphia but now part of the city, was the first German settlement, but most of the Germans became farmers. They took their produce either to Germantown or Philadelphia and, later, as Pennsylvania expanded, to nearby towns such as Lancaster, Reading, Easton, Bethlehem, Chester, and York, from which they were shipped mostly to Philadelphia. Although meat products, fruits, and vegetables were sold (as they still are at farmers' markets throughout the state), wheat soon became Pennsylvania's cash crop, which merchants bought and sold mostly to the West Indies. These colonies were the Arab Emirates of their day, although the most profitable product of the 1700s was sugar, not oil. Only small parcels of land there and in the eastern coast of Brazil and Guyana were fit to grow the sugar cane Europeans demanded to satisfy their tastes. Sugar was so profitable that it made sense economically to ship in food from the northern American colonies over a thousand miles away rather than to surrender the valuable sugar land to grow it. (It also made sense economically to import mostly male slaves from Africa, whose average life expectancy was only seven years, rather than to allow slaves to mate and produce families.)

Wars were fought between Holland, Spain, France, and Britain over who would control which island. By the 1760s, one-tenth of the members of the British Parliament derived their wealth from West Indian sugar plantations, and they were the wealthiest men in the empire. The American colonies were only supposed to trade with the British Islands, which swapped molasses (made into rum) and cash (to buy slaves in Africa or manufactured items—dishes, utensils, fancy clothes, books, etc.—in England) for wheat from Pennsylvania and New York and fish from New England. But of course they traded with whoever would buy wheat at a good price, and before the 1760s British customs collectors were as lax and corruptible as the Mexican officials who greet importers at the border today.

This international trade, managed by Philadelphia merchants and their British counterparts, was of course far from the mind of the Pennsylvania German farmers who were simply concerned with growing enough food to live on, plus a surplus to buy desired imports. Besides their work, they devoted themselves to preserving their faith and their way of life. And they were remarkably successful on both counts. Colonial Pennsylvania became famous for its prosperity as "the best poor man's country," and the mark the Pennsylvania Germans left on the cultural landscape remains among the most fascinating in the nation.

Unlike the Lutherans and Reformed, the German sectarians were pacifists, rejected infant baptism, lived simply, and kept to themselves. With the exception of the large Ephrata Cloister and the Moravians, they governed themselves in small congregations that handled disputes without resorting to courts. Most

Amish Barn Raising

numerous were the Mennonites, or Church of the Brethren as they are known today, named after their founder Menno Simons. In the 1690s, a more strict group, the Amish (begun by Jacob Ammon) separated from them. They are famous for refusing to use electricity or automobiles, and (unlike contemporary Mennonites) dress in distinctive, traditional clothes. Married men grow long beards. The Schwenkfelders were unique in that they embraced rather than shunned booklearning as did the other sects. The Dunkards (German Baptist Brethren) distinctively baptized their members by dunking them three times face forward into a flowing stream as they believed Jesus had done. Breaking off from the Dunkers in 1728, Conrad Beissel began the Ephrata Community, which he ruled as a charismatic figure. Men and women lived in spartan accommodations: clothes were coarse and beds were boards barely a foot wide. The last three of these groups are now extinct, although the Ephrata Cloister is now a museum village.

The Pennsylvania Moravians (or Unitas Fratum, the United Brethren), on the other hand, belonged to a world-wide missionary church that sent its members from Europe to Asia, Africa, and South America. Unlike the other small groups of Germans, they were governed by bishops and clergy. They first

arrived in 1740, and from their still-standing, impressive American headquarters in Bethlehem, Moravians sent out more missionaries than any other Protestant religion. They were especially successful in converting Indians, and ultimately did so as far away as Alaska. Living in separate "choirs"—women were equal to men in every respect—

✧

Below: Johann Valentine Haidt, The First Fruits. This remarkable painting, executed about 1755, shows some of the peoples converted throughout the world by the Moravians.

*Above: A remarkable example of "fraktur,"
the art of the Pennsylvania Germans,
Eternal Life and Etermal Damnation,
executed around 1820. A group of sinners
are marching to hell, including a soldier
(indicating a pacifist probably did the
painting), musicians, fancily dressed men
and women, and a Jewish peddler. The
Whore of Babylon welcomes them. Good
people, on the other hand, take up the Cross
and ascend to Heaven.*

*Right: A 1840s view of Bethlehem, much as
it was in the colonial era, and the Bell
House, Bethlehem. Led by Count Nicholas
von Zinzendorf, the Moravians arrived in
Bethlehem in 1740. Many of their large and
attractive buildings still survive, as does
their school as the present Moravian
College. Men and women lived separately in
"choirs." They were noted for their
missionary efforts with the Indians and
beautiful choral music, some of which is
now available on CD.*

Moravians believed the Holy Ghost represented the female side of God's nature as Jesus did
the male. Like the Ephrata Cloister and the

Harmony Society (now extinct, founded by
George Rapp in the early 1800s) music was
an important part of the Moravians'
lives. Unlike the simple tunes composed
by Conrad Beissel, their music (some of
which has been recorded) employed
instruments and resembled the mid-
eighteenth century classical works of Mozart
and Haydn. Besides music, Pennsylvania
Germans made an artistic contribution with
fraktur, or illustrated documents. They frequently decorated birth and marriage certificates or furniture with beautiful images of
birds and flowers.

The Pennsylvania German heritage today
not only appears in the Amish and Moravians
who still live according to their traditional
ways, but in the fact that after three hundred
years of intense cultivation, much of southeastern Pennsylvania remains among the most
fertile agriculture territory in the world. The
German legacies of hard work, thriftiness, and
loyalty to church and family endure as key
elements of Pennsylvania's heritage.

BETHLEHEM, PA.
From the West

FRANKLIN'S PHILADELPHIA AND ITS OPULENT COUNTRYSIDE

By 1776, Philadelphia, founded in 1682, had some twenty-five thousand inhabitants and was the largest city in the new American nation. New York and Boston, founded over a half century earlier, had only 20,000 and 16,000, respectively. Why was this so? First, Pennsylvania had a richer hinterland—the agricultural region that traded with the city—because of its fertile fields and more southerly location. But Philadelphia also owed much to its people, who loved their city and made it into the cultural as well as the economic capital of British North America. A British visitor in 1765 called it "a great and noble city," and a Frenchman in the 1780s considered it America's "most beautiful city," where "you will find more well-educated men, more knowledge of politics, and literature, and more political and learned societies than anywhere else in the United States."

Credit first goes to William Penn. In 1666, the Great Fire of London destroyed nearly the entire old city, mostly made of wood. Penn was determined that would not happen to "The City of Brotherly Love," which is what Philadelphia means in Greek. Houses had to be made of brick. Streets were wide and laid out on America's first grid—unlike the random layout of old New York and Boston, which owed much to the paths cows took home from their pastures. In keeping with Quaker modesty, they were named after trees (Pine, Chestnut, Walnut, etc.) and numbered rather than honoring individuals or places. Penn planned his city to run between the Delaware and Schuylkill Rivers, between what is now South and Vine Streets. Although by the time of the Revolution settlement had scarcely reached Seventh Street, and what is now Broad Street was still a cow pasture, Penn was planning for a great metropolis. The wisdom of his vision appears in the fact that while colonial New York and Boston were destroyed by fire in the American Revolution, much of colonial Philadelphia remains. A walk down Third Street from Walnut to South, or a stroll down Elfreth's Alley —which claims to be "the oldest street in America"—indeed create the illusion of an eighteenth-century city.

While Benjamin Franklin has come to embody colonial Pennsylvania and Philadelphia, he was only one of many public-spirited individuals who pioneered that vital American institution—"the voluntary association" or self-help society. Actually, Franklin, who was born in Boston, simply introduced to Philadelphia many of the features of Boston life. As a boy he borrowed books from Reverend Cotton Mather's library; in Philadelphia he started the Library Company that still exists. Unlike the Free Libraries founded throughout Philadelphia, this is still a private "company" which "shareholders" may join for $200, although any serious researcher may use one of the nation's finest collections of old published materials. Franklin lacked a higher education: he started the "Junto" where young men such as himself could read books and discuss the issues they raised. Later, he was instrumental in founding the College of Philadelphia, which is now the University of Pennsylvania. Women did their part, too. Presiding over the equivalent of eighteenth-century Paris salons, Elizabeth Graeme Fergusson (known as "the most learned woman in America"), Milcah Martha

✧

American wing, Samuel Powel House, Third Street, Philadelphia. Now a museum, built in 1768, the Powel House was one of the largest and most elegant mansions in colonial Philadelphia. Mrs. Powel's portrait is on the wall. George Washington was a good friend of Powel and frequently stayed at his house.

COURTESY OF THE AUTHOR.

✧

Top, left: Old Swedes' Church, the oldest surviving church in Pennsylvania, "Gloria Dei," was constructed by Swedish Lutherans in 1700. It became an Episcopal Church in 1845 and may be visited at Christian Street and Delaware Avenue (Columbus Blvd.) in Philadelphia. WPA Poster, promoting tourism, c. 1936-1941.
COURTESY OF THE LIBRARY OF CONGRESS.

Top, right: Philadelphia—Christ Church. The tallest building in colonial British North America at 196 feet, Christ Church, built in 1741, was the parish church of Bishop William White, who founded the Episcopal Church in the United States. Benjamin Franklin and Robert Morris, signers of the Declaration of Independence, owned pews there, and Franklin is buried in its graveyard.
COURTESY OF THE AUTHOR.

Below: Grist Mill at Burnt Cabins (now in Fulton County). In the 1750s, in an effort to keep recent settlers from disturbing the Indians, the Pennsylvania government burned their cabins. The settlers came back, the French and Indian War broke out, and this eighteenth century grist mill (one of over 2,000 mills in Pennsylvania by 1800, mostly grist mills that ground corn and wheat for local consumption and export) still survives.
COURTESY OF THE AUTHOR.

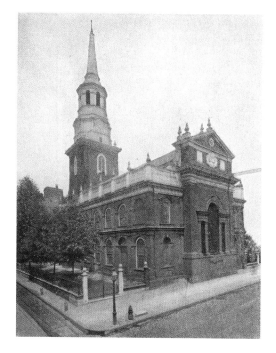

Moore, Susanna Wright, and Hannah Griffitts wrote and exchanged original essays and poetry that scholars only now are bringing to light. In what is now West Philadelphia, John Bartram, the nation's foremost botanist, exhibited plants he gathered from his extensive travels; his house still stands as part of a park.

Paved streets, a fire company, the nation's first College of Physicians and Surgeons, the Pennsylvania Hospital, the American Philosophical Society: all were in place by the American Revolution. Modeled on the British Royal Society, the elected members of the American Philosophical Society discussed, pursued, and published the latest advances in science and the life of the mind in general.

Philadelphia also boasted the tallest building in the American colonies, Christ Church, an Anglican house of worship, at 196 feet tall. Wealthy Philadelphians built beautiful country homes to escape the summer heat, some with names like Lemon Hill and Strawberry Hill. Many still exist as museums.

Yet for most of its citizens, Philadelphia was not a paradise. Of a cross-section of twenty Philadelphians at the time of the Revolution, three or four were servants or slaves, six were sailors or unskilled laborers, seven were artisans (most of whom were poorly paid assistants), one performed services (barber, clerk, etc.), one was a shopkeeper, one a merchant, and one a government official or professional person. Well-to-do Philadelphians did not remain indifferent. In 1768, private citizens founded a Bettering House where over six hundred men, women, and children worked each year at spinning and shoemaking to earn their keep. Another 350 were treated each year on average at the Pennsylvania Hospital for the Sick Poor, founded in 1751. Churches also distributed relief. Still, people without property, many of whom were homeless vagrants, committed several hundred crimes per year, mostly assault, theft, and disorderly conduct. In short, Philadelphia had all the troubles as well as the virtues of a modern city. Though only the sturdy brick houses and public buildings survive, we should remember that they do not tell the whole story.

BENJAMIN FRANKLIN

Today we remember him mostly as "Ben"—the poor boy who arrived in Philadelphia with a loaf of bread under each arm who worked his way up to be one of the world's great men—a statesman, writer, scientist, and public-spirited citizen. "The first downright American," writer D. H. Lawrence called him and indeed, his story resembles a folk tale like Dick Whittington (the poor boy who became Mayor of London) more than the biography of any other Founding Father. Only Franklin, of all the leaders who brought the United States into being, was ever an unfree laborer; he was indentured as a servant to his brother James, a Boston printer, a cantankerous man who drove him to run far enough away so he wouldn't be caught—to Philadelphia.

Born in 1706, the seventh son of a shoemaker, Franklin loved learning as a boy but his father could not afford to send him to the only college in Massachusetts at the time—Harvard. He expressed his feelings when he wrote the "Silence Dogood Letters" to his brother's newspaper, *The New England Courant*. "Silence" was an elderly woman who observed the college, where a gate-keeper only allowed those with money to enter, and from which many emerged "dunces and block-heads as before." Throughout his life, Franklin in his writings would assume the role of the under-dog—a scorned unmarried woman (Polly Baker), a "mulatto gentleman," a "Plainman" (making fun of the "better sort"), and most famously, "Poor Richard," under whose name he wrote an almanac from 1733 to 1758.

Despite his shortcomings, James Franklin did teach Ben the printer's trade. After a quick trip to England in his late teens, Ben returned as one of only three skilled printers in Philadelphia, and by far the best. As early as 1730 he was publishing all the official government documents. Soon there-after he took over what was then the province's one and only newspaper, *The Pennsylvania Gazette*. Having seen all different sorts of almanacs in England—scientific ones for the educated, comic ones for ordinary folk, even women's almanacs that discussed household items—he synthesized the best of each. *Poor Richard's Almanac* was a bestseller not only in Pennsylvania, but through part-ners Franklin trained in South Carolina and the West Indies as well.

✧

Franklin's Return to Philadelphia 1785, *by Jean L. G. Ferris, a nineteenth-century French artist. Also shown are Richard Bache and his wife, Franklin's daughter, Sarah, and her son, Benjamin Franklin Bache. Judge Thomas McKean stands at the right. Two African-American porters prepare to carry the aged Franklin in a sedan chair.* COURTESY OF THE LIBRARY OF CONGRESS.

FROM A MURAL PAINTING BY CHARLES E. MILLS, IN FRANKLIN UNION, BOSTON   COPR. THE FRANKLIN FOUNDATION

THOSE WHO WOULD GIVE UP ESSENTIAL LIBERTY FOR A LITTLE TEMPORARY SAFETY, DESERVE NEITHER LIBERTY NOR SAFETY.

WE MUST ALL HANG TOGETHER OR ASSUREDLY WE SHALL ALL HANG SEPARATELY.

D71539   BENJAMIN FRANKLIN SIGNING THE DECLARATION OF INDEPENDENCE   COPR. DETROIT PUBLISHING CO.

✧

Right: A mural by Charles E. Mills, showing Franklin signing the Declaration of Independence, with two of his more famous quotations below. John Hancock sits in the chair, Thomas Jefferson sits behind Franklin. This mural is located in the Franklin Union, Boston, one of two institutions, the other being the Franklin Institute, Philadelphia, founded with money from Franklin's estate to further technical and practical education.
COURTESY OF THE AUTHOR.

Bottom, right: Thirty-ton white marble statue of Franklin at the entrance to the Franklin Institute by James Earle Fraser. The bust of Franklin here was used for the 1/2¢ postage stamp in the 1938 "Presidents" series.
COURTESY OF THE AUTHOR.

Below: Currier and Ives poster of Benjamin Franklin, 1847.
COURTESY OF THE LIBRARY OF CONGRESS.

At the age of forty-two, Franklin's wealth enabled him to retire from business. About this time he had his first portrait painted—with a wig and elegant waistcoat, he dressed like the gentleman he aspired to be, rather than the worker he had been. But for the first time, in 1748, he found himself drawn into politics. Previously, his efforts on behalf of the public—paving streets, forming libraries and fire companies—were uncontroversial. Organizing a voluntary self-defense force to combat a possible French or Spanish invasion during King George's War was not, as many Quakers thought Pennsylvania had been spared the ravages of war because it refused even refused volunteers. Franklin entered the fray when the French and Indian War broke out, recruiting wagons and buying supplies for the British army, and then organizing Pennsylvania troops. When Proprietor Thomas Penn refused to pay taxes, in 1758 the Assembly sent Franklin to England as province agent to represent the colony in its efforts to become a royal colony.

Pennsylvania never became a royal colony, but Franklin became the most famous American in the world. Several other colonies chose him as their agent as well, the man to whom the British turned to learn "American opinion" when the Stamp, Townsend, and Tea Acts to raise revenue met with fierce resistance. Franklin was also famous for his electrical experiments—he discovered positive and negative charges. From 1758 until 1775, except for two years, he was America's spokesman in Europe, proof that the new land could produce an authentic genius.

Franklin never abandoned America's cause while overseas. Upon his return, he was elected to the Continental Congress, helped write the Declaration of Independence, and in 1778 went to France to negotiate the alliance that won the war. Coming back once more, he was a benign presence at the Constitutional Convention in 1787, calming the younger delegates down when their debates grew too heated. His final speech (James Wilson read all his speeches for him) was widely publicized and helped secure adoption of the Constitution. He argued that while neither he nor anyone else could agree with every aspect of the new government, no better document could have obtained a consensus.

Franklin spent the last four years of his life productively. He trained his grandson, Benjamin Franklin Bache, as a printer: the young man published the *Aurora*, the leading newspaper in America that supported Thomas Jefferson and opposed the Federalists in the 1790s. He sat in his front yard with the model of a bridge Thomas Paine had designed to span the Schuylkill River, urging that it be built to develop the Pennsylvania economy. Last but not least, he served as President of the American Anti-Slavery Society. His final published writing took on the person of an Arab who had captured some Americans trading in the Mediterranean Sea, and used the same arguments to enslave them (that they needed to be civilized, learn good work habits, and acquire the true religion) that American slave-owners used to justify enslaving blacks. In his will, Franklin left a legacy that after two hundred years (in 1990) would be used by the cities of Boston and Philadelphia to teach useful trades to poor boys. Franklin's disposal of his wealth, and his activities during his final years, make it abundantly clear that he realized America's greatness lay in providing for all the sort of opportunity he himself had enjoyed when he first showed up in Philadelphia with two loaves of bread.

THE FRENCH AND INDIAN WAR

Fort Necessity. Ten miles east of Uniontown, Pennsylvania on U. S. Route 40 (the National Road built with federal funds in the 1820s). Twenty-two-year-old Colonel George Washington's first military command ended in failure. In 1754, Virginia sent him into what is now southwestern Pennsylvania to claim the area and remove French and Indian forces who were also trying to control. The present structure is a faithful reconstruction of the original, tiny fort. It was built in 1954 to commemorate its 200th anniversary. Washington's defeat angered British officials who sent a large army to America the following year under General Edward Braddock, thus beginning the French and Indian War in America and starting a world war involving all the major European powers that did not end until 1763.

COURTESY OF THE AUTHOR.

While Pennsylvania avoided war from 1682 until 1755, its frontier expansion was increasingly troubled. In 1737, the Delawares in the northeastern part of the state agreed to give the province land equal to the territory a man could walk in one day, the infamous "Walking Purchase." Instead, the Pennsylvania government hired men who could run quickly, spread them out at intervals, and thereby laid claim to a large region. Along with Indians on the western frontier, in the Juniata Valley, who objected to removal, the Delaware were kept in line by the Iroquois. Happy to have a peaceful, unthreatening Pennsylvania on their southern border, the Iroquois were the enforcers who enabled Pennsylvania to "peacefully" expand westward. In turn, the Pennsylvania government burned out its own settlers—from the "Burnt Cabins" area of the Juniata—to ensure that the Indians protected by the Iroquois retained possession of their own lands.

✧

Above: Life of George Washington, the Soldier. Lithograph of a painting by Junius Brutus Stearns showing the young Washington, on horseback, fighting at the battle where General Braddock's forces were attacked and decimated, near present-day Pittsburgh.

COURTESY OF THE LIBRARY OF CONGRESS.

Below: Conrad Weiser (1696-1760), who was the principal frontier mediator between Pennsylvania and the western Indians in the 1740s and 1750s, saw his work dashed during the French and Indian War. His cabin survives as a state historical site in Womelsdorf on Route 422 west of Reading.

COURTESY OF THE AUTHOR.

Keeping Indians and Europeans separate became increasingly difficult as large numbers of Scots-Irish from Northern Ireland began to come to Pennsylvania in the 1740s in response to economic hard times. With nearly all the good land in the east already owned, they headed west and south, some down the Shenandoah Valley to settle the backcountry of Virginia and the Carolinas, but others to western Pennsylvania. Unlike the German sectarians, they were not peaceful. And in the west, they found three other claimants for the same territory: Indians, French Canadians, and Virginians.

Unlike the Pennsylvania government, both the French and the Virginians sought to obtain military control over the region, especially the crucial point where the Allegheny and the Monongahela rivers met to form the Ohio. The French arrived there first and built Fort Duquesne. In 1754, a twenty-two-year-old Virginia army colonel, George Washington, tried to challenge them, but met defeat at Fort Necessity (which has been reconstructed on its original site.)

Washington had no idea at the time that he had started a world war. For the first time, the British government, instead of ignoring a frontier border dispute with its traditional enemy, the French, decided to support the Americans and drive the French out of Canada once and for all. The first expedition it sent, in 1755, under General James Braddock, was a disaster. Over 2,000 British and Virginia colonial troops were ambushed shortly before reaching Pittsburgh, having marched from Williamsburg, Virginia. Braddock's defeat signaled Indians in the Ohio Valley, who had been displaced from Pennsylvania over the past forty years, to try to regain their territories. Attacking all along the frontier, they drove settlers back across the Susquehanna and inflicted some three thousand deaths. Bethlehem, Lancaster, and Reading became centers for refugees; raids went as far east as the Delaware River, at one point to Port Jervis, New York. Meanwhile, war had broken out in Europe. Britain, led by William Pitt, and Prussia, led by Frederick the Great, fought Austria, Russia, France, and (later) Spain. Britain's money and enormous navy, combined with Frederick's well-trained soldiers, enabled these two smaller nations to defeat rivals many times their size.

Meanwhile, Pennsylvania was responding resourcefully to the crisis. In 1756, eight pacifist Quaker deputies resigned from the Assembly, leaving the Quaker party in control of its members who did not flinch from hostilities. The province then built forty forts, mostly large loghouses, stretching from the Delaware Water Gap to the Juniata Valley, where the widely dispersed farmers could gather for protection. Then an expedition led by Lieutenant Colonel John Armstrong attacked and defeated the Delawares at their encampment at Kittanning on the Allegheny River. Pennsylvania also contributed twenty-seven hundred volunteers to General John Forbes' expedition, which left Carlisle in July 1758 and arrived at Fort Duquesne that November after cutting what is still known as "Forbes Road" through the wilderness. Rather than surrender, the French blew up the fort, which was rebuilt, named Fort Pitt, and the town around it Pittsburgh.

Meanwhile, the British were doing their part, sending expeditions to New York and Canada annually from 1756 to 1759, the year James Wolfe conquered Quebec. But warfare had not

The Home of Conrad Weiser, Womelsdorf, Penn'a.
Indian Interpreter During Colonial Period.

ended on the Pennsylvania frontier. In 1763, the Ottawa Chief Pontiac and his spiritual leader Neolin unified various Indian nations and launched a major assault on western Pennsylvania, besieging Fort Pitt. Colonel Henry Bouquet marched against them leading Pennsylvania volunteers, circulating blankets infected with smallpox among the Indians. He defeated the Indians at the Battle of Bushy Run near Pittsburgh, and in 1764 marched his force through the Ohio Valley, compelling Pontiac to retreat further west.

Yet although the French and Indian war was a success for the British and their colonies, it left a bitter aftertaste in Pennsylvania. Believing the colony's government, overwhelmingly dominated by easterners, had failed to defend them, the Paxton Boys, who lived in the region of present-day Harrisburg, marched on Lancaster and took out their frustrations by massacring a peaceful community of Conestoga Indians who had been converted by the Moravians. They then marched on Philadelphia, where Benjamin Franklin, temporarily back from England, led a force that met them at Germantown and promised to protect them in the future. They finally returned home, although some moved to northern Pennsylvania, where they would fight Connecticut settlers who laid claim to that region.

The French and Indian War marked the end of William Penn's "Holy Experiment." The world's only government that had tried to live without military defense was finally forced to fight. Eastern and western Pennsylvania mistrusted each other, the former wanting peace with the Indians, the latter desiring to defend the frontier. These tensions, and others, would reappear during the American Revolution, ensuring that not only would Pennsylvanians fight for independence against Britain, but would also struggle fiercely among themselves over who was to rule Pennsylvania.

✧

George Washington Crossing the Delaware. *A simplified version of the painting by Emanuel Leutze. Washington and his men used Pennsylvania Durham boats to make the journey from what is now Washington Crossing, Pennsylvania—site of a museum, park, and David Library of the American Revolution—to a spot near Trenton, New Jersey. Washington could not have stood erect in the boat in this manner and kept his balance.*

THE AMERICAN REVOLUTION

In May, 1776, two months before the Declaration of Independence was signed, Congress, meeting in Philadelphia, adopted John Adams' resolution that "where no government sufficient to the exigencies of affairs existed," the people should adopt a new one "best conducive to their happiness and safety." Congress did this largely out of exasperation with Pennsylvania's Proprietor John Penn and the Pennsylvania Assembly, which had refused to select delegates to the Continental Congress in the first place. Congress met at Carpenters' Hall, rather than the State House, to acknowledge that the real enthusiasm for the

PHILADELPHIA

CARPENTERS' HALL

FEDERAL ART PROJECT W.P.A. PENNSYLVANIA

✧

Above: Carpenter's Hall. The First Continental Congress met in Carpenter's Hall, built in 1724, rather than the Pennsylvania assembly's home (next door) to show their approval of working class Philadelphians who supported strong resistance to Britain rather than the conservative Pennsylvania legislature.

COURTESY OF THE LIBRARY OF CONGRESS.

Below: The Betsy Ross House in Philadelphia as it appeared around 1908. Built in 1740, the official website notes "it is believed that Betsy Ross lived here from 1773 to 1785" and that she made the first official American flag at this site. For the 1876 Centennial Exposition, the Mund family, which operated it as a tavern at the time, advertised it as the "Original Flag House, Lager, Wine and Liquors. This is the house where the first United States flag was made by Mrs. John Ross." It became a museum in 1937.

COURTESY OF THE AUTHOR.

Revolution in Pennsylvania came from the working people of Philadelphia and informal organizations throughout the province. The Committee of Privates, representing rank-and-file soldiers in Philadelphia, and Committees of Associators everywhere were recruiting soldiers, enforcing Congress' boycott of British goods, and obtaining supplies and money for the Continental Army, which had formed almost a year before.

Unlike the Massachusetts House of Representatives or Virginia House of Burgesses, the Pennsylvania Assembly never endorsed independence; it went out of existence in September, 1776 after it had become meaningless. The Assembly was so conservative because in the 1760s and 1770s as other colonies were standing up for their rights, Pennsylvania's two parties were courting the King and Parliament: the Quaker Party was trying to have Pennsylvania's proprietors, the Penn family, replaced by a royal government, while the Proprietary party was trying to show how well they had maintained loyalty as opposed to elsewhere. The Assembly was dominated by the three oldest counties—Bucks, Chester, and Philadelphia—which numbered less than half the province by the 1770s but sent 24 of 30 delegates to the legislature. They were heavily Quaker, English, Anglican, wealthy, conservative, and contented.

The western counties and the Philadelphia workingmen were not. For them, the cry of "Taxation without Representation" applied just as much to the Pennsylvania government as to distant England. They had not forgotten how long it took the Assembly to vote funds to protect the frontier—that is, push out the Indians. As the Revolution would show, Indians were still a real threat in the Wyoming Valley (around Wilkes-Barre) and in the west near Pittsburgh. While the older counties contained numerous loyalists and pacifist Germans and Quakers, the interior counties of Lancaster, Berks, York, Northampton, and Cumberland were the first outside New England to respond to Congress' call for troops to join George Washington outside Boston following the Battle of Bunker Hill. These counties, which boasted numerous iron furnaces and gunsmiths, supplied the Pennsylvania riflemen who were a mainstay of the Continental line throughout the war.

Similarly, since the Philadelphia elite supplied no fervent revolutionaries on the order of Patrick

Henry or John Hancock, new men took the lead. Scientist David Rittenhouse (whose planetarium is still on display at the University of Pennsylvania), painter Charles Willson Peale, indebted merchants Charles Thomson ("the Sam Adams of Philadelphia") and Timothy Matlack (a "fighting Quaker"), and mathematics professor James Cannon took their places. Most spectacularly of all, a former British tax collector, Thomas Paine, arrived in Philadelphia in late 1775 and penned *Common Sense*, a call for American independence, in January, 1776. Claiming that the palaces of kings were built on the ruins of paradise, he urged America to become for all the world—as indeed it had been for him—an asylum for lovers of liberty. Returning from England as the revolutionaries' titular head was Benjamin Franklin, who became the first president of the state of Pennsylvania under the constitution drafted by delegates chosen by the associators in September, 1776.

The new constitution horrified moderate revolutionaries. Nearly all power was vested in the Assembly, which was elected by all taxpaying males. To accompany this very democratic feature was an equally undemocratic one—only people who swore an oath on a Christian bible to the new government were eligible to vote, eliminating loyalists, Quakers, pacifists, and those revolutionaries who thought men of wealth ought to be represented in an upper house, as in most of the states. In the nation's first experiment with rotation in office, assemblymen could only be elected four years out of seven. To make sure their representatives did not go against the people's will, all laws (except those required by emergencies) had to be taken back to the voters, discussed, and then passed again the following year. A Council of Censors was the only significant check on the Assembly; it could recommend to the voters that laws be disallowed as unconstitutional or simply unwise.

In practice, the new government had problems from the start. Attempting to keep merchants from profiting too much from rising prices, crowds in Philadelphia intimidated wealthy men and accused them of loyalism. People refused to pay the high taxes required by war. The northern third of Pennsylvania was claimed by the state of Connecticut, the southwestern corner by Virginia. Connecticut "Yankees" siding with the Revolution

Washington at Valley Forge, *by E. Percy Moran, c. 1911. Washington's Headquarters at Valley Forge.*

COURTESY OF THE LIBRARY OF CONGRESS.

fought pro-British "Pennamites" allied with the Iroquois in the Wyoming Valley in a ferocious guerrilla conflict.

Both the American and British armies came to Pennsylvania in 1776. On Christmas Eve, George Washington's army, headquartered along the Delaware River at the location now named "Washington Crossing," rowed across the ice-choked water and surprised a Hessian garrison at Trenton, New Jersey. Washington had been forced to evacuate New York that summer and chased across New Jersey. This vital victory over a small force provided the morale boost that meant enough soldiers would reenlist on January 1, 1777, to keep the Continental Army in the field. In the summer of 1777, General Sir William Howe took about half his army from New York and attacked Philadelphia in September, after sailing all the way south around the eastern shore of Maryland and up Chesapeake Bay. Howe feared an ambush on land in New Jersey, and powerful American forts and underwater defenses on the Delaware River. He managed to occupy the city after defeating the Americans first at Brandywine and then at Germantown, but Washington's troops acquitted themselves well, inflicted as many casualties as they suffered, and withdrew in good order.

With Philadelphia as with New York, the British could occupy a city that the Royal Navy could supply from the sea, but they could neither control nor obtain adequate provisions from the countryside. Washington chose his 1777 winter quarters at Valley Forge so that he had easy access to supplies of food and arms from the rich interior of Pennsylvania, and also because the cliffs commanded the Schuylkill River and were impregnable from a British attack. There Baron Von Steuben drilled the Continentals to the point that when French generals first encountered Washington's troops in 1780, they could admire an American army equal to their own. News of the French alliance of 1778 compelled the British to withdraw from Philadelphia; they had to send much of their forces to the West Indies to fight for these rich sugar islands the French coveted.

Although Pennsylvania's frontiers suffered greatly during the war, the heart of the province—the rich grain-producing interior counties that also manufactured guns, cannons, and wagons—and the city of Philadelphia—emerged from the conflict in good shape. Pennsylvania was poised to lead the new nation into a healthy economic and political future.

THE DECLARATION OF INDEPENDENCE AND THE UNITED STATES CONSTITUTION

No history of Pennsylvania would be complete without telling the story of the two fundamental documents of American history that were written, eleven years apart, and are now commemorated at Independence Hall National Park.

Nearly everything we think we know about the Declaration of Independence isn't quite correct. It was not adopted unanimously, although it claimed to be (Pennsylvania's John Dickinson refused to sign and the New York delegates were ordered not to by their state); it was not signed on July 4 in the impressive ceremony made famous by John Trumbull's painting, but rather approved on July 2, and signed by everyone except John Hancock after July 4; it was left on the front desk and men signed when they felt like it.

Nor is the Declaration's meaning clear. "All men are created equal and endowed with certain inalienable rights, and among these are life, liberty, and the pursuit of happiness" has been the source for arguments among citizens, politicians, and political thinkers ever since loyalist critics pointed out at once that many of the signers owned slaves, and that Britain had abolished slavery on its home territory (although not in its colonies) four years earlier. On one level, the Declaration simply means that every nation has an equal right to govern itself, and that therefore America has an equal right to pursue its destiny (under whatever political arrangements it chooses) with Britain. Declaring independence made the cause for which men had been fighting for over a year clear: previously, they had been shooting at troops sent by a king to whom they claimed to be loyal. Another main purpose of the Declaration was to announce to the French and the Spanish—who had no use for the Americans' popular governments but wished to humiliate their traditional enemy, the British—that they would not abandon the war, reconcile with the Mother Country, and leave their European allies in the lurch. Much of the Declaration is a list of grievances—among them taxation, failure to allow colonies to extend representation to western regions, and sending soldiers to Boston and closing up the harbor in response to the Tea Party colonies.

But the phrase "all men are created equal" began to take on a wider meaning almost at once. Charles Carroll, the only Roman Catholic to sign the Declaration, hoped that Americans, to be true to their principles, would give people of his religion the right to vote and hold office. Most states eventually expanded the right to vote to all male, white taxpayers; revolutionaries began to free their slaves, and all the states north of Maryland passed laws to gradually end slavery—Pennsylvania being the first in 1780. In 1848, American women met at Seneca Falls, New York, and declared that "all men and women are created equal" before proceeding to list women's grievances against men, much as the Declaration had listed the ways George III had antagonized the colonies. Thomas Jefferson, shortly before he died on the fiftieth anniversary of the traditionally agreed upon day that the Declaration was adopted, July 4, 1826, put it best:

"May it be to the world…the signal of arousing men to burst their chains…and assume the blessings of self-government. The form which we have…restores the free right to the unbounded exercise of reason and freedom of opinion. All eyes are opened or opening to the rights of man…. The mass of mankind has not been born with saddles on their backs nor a favored few, booted and spurred, ready to ride them legitimately, by Grace of God. These are grounds for hope for others; for ourselves, let the annual return of this day forever refresh our recollections of these rights, and an undiminished devotion to them."

The United States Constitution, drafted during the hot summer of 1787 in the Pennsylvania State House, owes far more to the state of Pennsylvania than its mere location. In order for the Constitution to be approved, five things had to happen: Congress had to approve a call to revise the Articles of Confederation under which the nation had been governed during the Revolution; state legislatures had to send delegates to the Constitutional Convention; the Convention had to agree on a document; the state legislatures had to approve the call for state conventions to ratify the Constitution; and then nine out of thirteen state conventions had to approve it. Pennsylvania was the second state (Delaware was the first) and first large one to endorse the Constitution, but it was a close call. The anti-federalists who opposed the Constitution had two votes more than the one-third required to block the Pennsylvania Assembly from approving a ratifying convention. They simply refused to show up for the vote, as approval of the Convention required two-thirds of the entire legislature whether all members were present or not. Philadelphia Federalists responded by locating two anti-Federalists, physically bringing them to the state house, and keeping them there so the vote could be taken. Pennsylvania's ratifying convention then approved the Constitution by a vote of 46-23 after the Constitution was thoroughly debated in newspapers and pamphlets throughout the state.

But even Pennsylvania anti-federalists made an important contribution to the Constitution. Led by Robert Whitehill, John Smilie, and William Findley, men whose names should be better known, they put forward fifteen objections which circulated throughout the states that became the first proposals for what became the Bill of Rights. Freedom of religion, trial by jury, protection against cruel and unusual punishment and unauthorized search and seizure, freedom of speech and the press, the right to bear arms, and the preservation of states' rights were all advanced during the constitutional debates by Pennsylvania anti-federalists. The Federalists' willingness to support the Bill of Rights, which passed the first Congress in 1791 and was soon ratified by the states, satisfied most anti-federalists that the new government did not threaten personal or community liberties. Thus, the anti-federalist contribution ensured that the Constitution and new government were welcomed by a united nation, rather than by the Federalists alone.

✧

Above: Thomas Paine, 1737-1809, painted by the famous British artist George Romney in 1794. Paine's two greatest writings, Common Sense, *published in 1776 in Philadelphia which urged Americans to abandon monarchy, and* The Rights of Man, *which supported the the French Revolution and was published in London in 1793, are on the table to his right.*
COURTESY OF THE LIBRARY OF CONGRESS.

ECONOMIC AND RELIGIOUS
DEVELOPMENTS IN THE EARLY REPUBLIC

Pennsylvania did more than stand at the center of politics in the early republic. The state was becoming an economic powerhouse. Pennsylvania's grain production and iron manufacturers flourished during and after the War for Independence, and Philadelphia merchants made fortunes as privateers, capturing British vessels and bringing foreign merchandise to port. During the Revolution, in 1780, Superintendent of Public Finance Robert Morris and ninety-two Philadelphia merchants founded the Bank of Pennsylvania, the first in the United States. They raised over £300,000 to support a national government that was relying on inflated paper money to pay its debts. The Bank of the United States followed in 1781. Combined with the Society for the Encouragement of Manufacturers—created in 1787 to offer bounties for new technology and specifically to compete with the British textile industry that dominated American markets—Pennsylvania had implemented on a state level the essence of the financial program Alexander Hamilton proposed to the new nation in 1790. (Morris, in fact, was George Washington's first choice for secretary of the Treasury.)

Pennsylvania's economy produced a number of "firsts" for America. In 1783, Morris and his partners outfitted the first American ship to reach the Far East, *The Empress of China*. It began the famous "China trade" and led to thriving American trade to India and the South Pacific. As the Constitutional Convention met in the summer of 1787, the delegates took time off to observe the nation's first steamboat, designed by John Fitch to navigate the Delaware. Although Robert Fulton—himself a native of Lancaster, Pennsylvania—usually receives the credit for inventing the first successful steamboat, he did not. From 1787 to 1790, three boats Fitch developed connected Burlington, New Jersey with Philadelphia before he went out of business. He then traveled to Kentucky, where he failed to make his way, and committed suicide in 1798. Philadelphia was also the site of the nation's first labor union and strike (the Franklin typographers in 1786), stock exchange (1791), insurance company (1792), and paved intercity road (the Philadelphia-Lancaster Turnpike, 1794). As Governor Thomas Mifflin urged in his 1789 inaugural address as the state's first governor under the new constitution, Pennsylvanians should "persevere in improvements of every kind…. Consider Pennsylvania…as a natural avenue from the shores of the Atlantic to the vast regions of the western territory. Imagination can hardly paint the magnitude of the scene which demands our industry, nor hope exaggerate the richness of the reward which solicits our enjoyment."

The Revolution produced religious changes, too. Required by their ordination oaths to swear allegiance to the King of England, every Pennsylvania Anglican minister except one—William White of Christ and St. Peter's United Churches, Philadelphia—either moved to England or ceased holding services. Aware the church was in trouble because of these loyalist inclinations, White organized a series of conferences between 1784 and 1789 that led to the creation of the American Episcopal Church with White as the first presiding American bishop—with the blessing of the British clergy. On the other hand, the British bishops refused to recognize those ministers nominated by John Wesley, who had not formally been ordained as priests and whose highly emotional preaching offended Anglicans who preferred more ritual in their services and reasoned arguments in their sermons. This led the Methodists to split off from the Episcopal Church that had formerly been their home. Also after the Revolution, the Unitarians (who denied the Holy Trinity) and Universalists (who believed everyone would be saved), denominations that later joined together, emerged. By the Civil War, one-third of all Americans were Methodists, one-sixth Unitarian Universalists.

William White not only organized the Episcopal Church; in 1794, he made an important contribution to black Christianity by ordaining Absalom Jones as the first black deacon, and later priest, in the United States. Jones' church, St. Thomas', opened shortly before Mother Bethel of the African Methodist Episcopal Church, founded by his friend Richard Allen. In the years after the Revolution, Philadelphia developed the nation's first middle-class African-American community. Guided by former slaves like Allen and Jones whose masters freed them and whose powerful preaching made them community leaders, the city's blacks flocked to these congregations where they governed themselves and were not segregated or excluded as in most of the white churches.

The American Revolution was more than a struggle that affected men. It created opportunities for women, who began to attend academies where they received an education equal to men at colleges, and where some put forward the radical idea that they were entitled to political rights. But most women accepted their new role as guardians of republican liberty and educators of the next generation. Still, in 1781, Esther DeBerdt Reed, whose husband Joseph was then President of Pennsylvania, organized the first political activity by women in the American nation—raising money from wealthy women to help the bankrupt nation. Flagmaker Betsy Ross was not the only Pennsylvania woman to make revolutionary history.

✧

Refugees of various sorts, including revolutionaries such as scientist Joseph Priestley, future King Louis Philippe of France, and hundreds of blacks from Haiti, came to Pennsylvania in the 1790s. Some French royalists hoped to rescue Queen Marie Antoinette of France after King Louis XVI was executed in 1793 and establish a court in exile in northern Pennsylvania at Azilum ("asylum"). Some of the original buildings remain in this beautiful setting.

Top: The Chestnut Street Theatre opened in Philadelphia in 1793. George Washington frequently attended. The theatre was destroyed by fire in 1820. This print is by William Birch, whose many attractive drawings frequently appear in books to illustrate life in Philadelphia.

Middle: Albert Gallatin's Mansion, "Friendship Hill." Built in 1789 near present New Geneva in Western Pennsylvania, the rise of this Swiss immigrant as America's first significant glass manufacturer, community leader, and ultimately Secretary of the Treasury under Presidents Jefferson and Madison demonstrates the economic mobility and quickly developing prosperity of Pennsylvania's frontier in the early republic.

Bottom: This mansion, Philadelphia's grandest, was built during the 1780s for Robert Morris, the financier of the American Revolution. George Washington lived there while he was President.

TWO REBELLIONS: WHISKEY AND FRIES

The national harmony which greeted George Washington's election as the nation's first president in 1789 was short-lived. In fact, the 1790s witnessed the United States' most bitter political struggle apart from the one that led to the Civil War. Two issues separated the Federalists, as the party led by Washington and Secretary of the Treasury Alexander Hamilton was known, and the Republicans (or Democrats) led by Secretary of State Thomas Jefferson. Hamilton proposed an ambitious program to create a national bank, pay off the state and national debt (some $70 million dollars) at face value, and promote commercial and industrial development. Jefferson feared this would jeopardize America's special position as a nation of property-owning farmers and create a moneyed aristocracy. The Republicans also looked favorably on the French Revolution, although not all of its excess bloodshed, as a worthy successor to our own. The Federalists believed instead that the United States needed to cultivate the friendship of Britain, by far its largest trading partner, and a much-needed force for order in a revolutionary age.

Pennsylvania was at the center of these disputes. Philadelphia was the national capital and its largest city from 1790 to 1800. It also was the center of the printing industry: John Fenno's Federalist *Gazette of the United States* competed with Benjamin Franklin Bache's Republican *Aurora* in slinging insults that today would make politicians blush. The Federalists termed the Republicans "Jacobins" after the bloody French faction that instituted the Reign of Terror, while the Republicans called the Federalists "Anglomaniacs." Neither side had come to accept the idea that a legitimate opposition party could exist, as opposed to a revolutionary organization or conspiracy that hoped to overthrow the government.

Pennsylvania political races were very tight in the 1790s. Whichever party could take Pennsylvania and New York would emerge triumphant, as New England was strongly Federalist, the South strongly Republican. Politics even came into play as doctors treated victims of the eight yellow fever epidemics that killed thousands of Philadelphians between 1793 and 1805. Federalist physicians insisted that French refugees from the Haitian Revolution infected the republic; Republicans blamed the city's unhealthy environment. (Actually, both were right; mosquitoes brought from the West Indies thrived in the swampy environs near the city.) As most of the government's leaders evacuated the city during the summers when the epidemics raged, Philadelphia's African Americans remained behind to care for the sick. Racist politicians accused them of doing it for the money, although they put their own lives at risk and the Free African Society that they began to care for each other's misfortunes went broke in the process.

But Pennsylvania's most notable response to these political struggles was two rebellions, launched by farmers to protest the taxes that Federalists required to pay the interest on the debt (which more than doubled the $3 million the government spent during its first year) and support an army with which they planned in 1798 both to attack French territories and suppress their critics at home. Pennsylvanians had managed to avoid paying state taxes throughout most of the 1780s and 1790s. The state met its revenue needs by selling off some of the expansive western lands that it owned and granting a good deal as well to Revolutionary War veterans to pay off the state debts.

The Whiskey Rebellion occurred during the summer of 1794. Congress had passed a tax of 25 percent on distilled whiskey, which provided western Pennsylvania farmers with much of their income, as it was unprofitable to ship solid corn across the state's mountainous terrain. It did not help that John Neville, a locally unpopular wealthy Virginian, was the region's principal tax collector. The trouble started when protestors erected liberty poles (as in the Revolution) and compelled tax collectors to resign, sometimes by tarring and feathering them. When Neville refused to quit his post, members of the Mingo Creek Democratic Society (these societies sprang up throughout the nation to support the French Revolution and oppose the Federalists) burned down his house following a battle in which four men died; two others were killed in the uprising. President Washington raised an army of over 12,000 men, marched at its head most of the way to Westmoreland County, and met no armed resistance. He pardoned those ringleaders who were captured.

Before the Whiskey Rebellion, western Pennsylvanians were angry that they were being taxed by a government that seemed not to care about their needs. Indian raids continued until the early 1790s as far as the vicinity of Pittsburgh: two armies sent to secure the frontier were defeated. Diplomacy had failed to open the port of New Orleans, the capital of Spanish Louisiana, to Americans, preventing them from sending their grain down the Mississippi River and selling it to Europe and the West Indies. But even as the Whiskey Rebellion was occurring, General Anthony Wayne—himself a Pennsylvanian from Chester County—defeated the Ohio Valley Indians at the Battle of Fallen Timbers, and the Treaty of Greenville in 1795 led to their withdrawal further west. The same year, Charles Pinckney negotiated the treaty with Spain that bears his name permitting American goods to descend the Mississippi. The westerners' grievances had been met.

Like the Whiskey uprising, Fries' "Rebellion" of 1799 only received that name from its enemies. The participants considered themselves people who resisted unfair taxation, and had no intention of overthrowing the government. In 1798, a Federalist-dominated Congress passed a "window tax" on real estate and personal property. Previously pro-Federalist Pennsylvania Germans in Berks and Northampton Counties led by John Fries resisted tax collectors by pouring hot water on their heads and destroying their records. They had to be rescued by volunteer companies from Philadelphia. President Adams pardoned Fries and others convicted of treason and lesser charges.

During the "Quasi-War of 1797-1800" when French and American ships battled each other, the Federalist party sealed its doom by passing the Alien and Sedition Acts. Allowing the president to deport undesirable aliens without a trial—many of his Republican critics were recent immigrants from the British Isles—and making "false" criticism of the government a crime turned most of the nation against a party that so flagrantly used national security as an excuse to violate civil liberties. Benjamin Franklin Bache died of yellow fever while awaiting trial for sedition; his successor, William Duane, was chased across Philadelphia rooftops by Federalists before being jailed. He was acquitted, although Thomas Cooper, editor of the *Sunbury and Northampton Gazette*, served six months in jail. Pennsylvania joined the nation in repudiating the Federalists in the election of 1800. By 1802, the party held no seats in the state's congressional delegation and state senate, and only 9 out of 86 in the assembly. Western Pennsylvanian Albert Gallatin, a glass manufacturer and leading opponent of the Federalists and their taxes, became Secretary of the Treasury under presidents Thomas Jefferson and James Madison, serving in that post for thirteen years, the longest in American history, before he joined the American diplomats in Europe who negotiated an end to the War of 1812. While the nation's capital moved to Washington, D. C., Pennsylvania financial know-how, both with Gallatin and later Nicholas Biddle as President of the Second Bank of the United States from 1819 to 1836, was critical to the new nation.

PENNSYLVANIA REFORM: PENITENTIARIES, THE TEMPERANCE MOVEMENT, AND WOMEN'S RIGHTS

For many Pennsylvanians and Americans, creating a new nation where people governed themselves was only the beginning. America had to show the world it could produce a superior order of human being, not only more self-reliant, but more moral, prosperous, and better educated than those under the sway of European monarchs. A republic could only survive, the Founding Fathers thought, if it contained virtuous citizens who cared more about their nation's liberty than their personal gain. At the center of nearly every reform was Pennsylvania physician Benjamin Rush.

Prison reform was of major concern to Rush. Traditionally, criminals were punished physically with whippings, public humiliation (the stocks or the pillory) and sometimes death for murder, armed robbery, and occasionally other crimes. Jails primarily were holding pens until the accused

came to trial, and only people who failed to pay their debts remained in them for long periods. (It was hoped their friends or family would come to their rescue, since only people with some wealth to begin with could obtain money on credit.) Rush took the lead in urging that the traditional jail be replaced with what are now called penitentiaries or reformatories. These words describe their new function: instead of merely punishing criminals, society would rehabilitate them by confining them for long periods and subjecting them to moral influences rather than the criminal elements who were mixed together in jails.

Pennsylvania led the nation in implementing this system. It reached its peak when the Eastern State Penitentiary, which now survives as a museum, was built in the Fairmount section of Philadelphia in 1829. With Niagara Falls and the huge factories where women labored in Lowell, Massachusetts, it became one of the nation's three biggest tourist attractions. Prisoners were kept in solitary confinement where they labored at trades and were permitted only a Bible and visits by clergymen and other people of high moral character. Charles Dickens, who visited America, believed the prison drove its inmates mad, but surprisingly most of those who were released never returned. The Pennsylvania system, as its was known, was copied throughout the state although other states preferred to keep prisoners in groups where they labored together.

Rush came to believe that alcohol was the root of most social evils. In the early 1800s, Americans drank about twice as much hard liquor, on average, as they do today. While he himself and many temperance reformers did not object to beer or wine, they urged that they be consumed in moderation. Rush invented a "moral thermometer" where people who consumed only water were rated highest and lived a healthy and productive life, while those who drank whiskey or rum to excess were doomed to an early death, poverty, and a life of crime. Although Pennsylvania never endorsed prohibition—it was not among the three-quarters of the states that ratified the Eighteenth Amendment in

1919—it attained many converts in the state. Some, unfortunately, gave up drinking so quickly that they died of shock.

Curing the insane was another concern. Rush and other reformers believed they should not simply be left alone or ignored, but that most could be restored to sanity. While he preferred gentle methods, Rush invented a restraining device that many of the new asylums used to keep patients immobile and in total darkness to calm them down when they behaved wildly. Where trained personnel could spend time with the mentally disturbed, they fared well, but all too often public asylums put low costs ahead of personal care for their inmates.

The new republic demanded a special role for women, too. Rush was one of the founders in 1787 of the Philadelphia Female Academy. Although not allowed to attend colleges, many academies offered women the same education available to men at colleges. The

✧

Above: Fairmount Water Works. Constructed between 1812 and 1819, visitors from Europe and the United States marveled at this beautiful structure, still surviving intact at the foot of the Art Museum on the Schuylkill River. The most advanced municipal water system in the world at the time, it was later decorated with gardens and became the starting point for Fairmount Park, founded in 1855.
COURTESY OF THE AUTHOR.

Below: An 1808 cartoon mocking Governor Simon Snyder, leader of the "clodhopper" Democrats, the first backcountry farmer to be elected to the state's highest office. The cartoon pretends to be "respectfully dedicated to all the butchers in the United States" but their comic appearance, that of the bull, and the presence of black fiddlers suggests anything but praise.
COURTESY OF THE LIBRARY OF CONGRESS.

GENERAL JACKSON SLAYING THE MANY HEADED MONSTER.

purpose was different, though. Women were supposed to be more moral than men, the guardians of virtue, children, and the home, the domestic as opposed to the public sphere. Not all of them accepted this willingly. During the 1790s, inspired by the politically active women of revolutionary France, some "fiery Frenchified dames" of Pennsylvania, as their critics called them, demanded equal political rights and insisted on being called "citess," the female form of citizen.

They did not succeed, but women were able to use the superior moral nature men attributed to them to attack moral evils, especially slavery, which they argued separated families and permitted men to ignore their wives to take advantage of their slaves. Similarly, they were especially active in the temperance movement, for men who drank neglected or abused their wives and children, in addition to spending money required for their support in taverns.

PENNSYLVANIA TRANSPORTATION

Even as Pennsylvanians were discovering their great natural resources of lumber, iron, coal, and oil, they were becoming aware of the main obstacle to using them: except for the fertile farmland of the southeastern part of the state, Pennsylvania is an almost endless series of mountain ranges separated by valleys and rivers, most of which are not (like New York's Hudson) easily navigable. A transportation revolution had to precede the industrial revolution. By the early 1800s, almost all Pennsylvanians regardless of their political position were firmly committed to internal improvements such as roads, bridges, canals, and railroads, differing mostly as to where they should be located, and whether public or private funds, loans or taxes, or a mixture of both should fund them.

The earliest roads in Pennsylvania were Indian trails. Given the mountainous terrain, narrow gaps, and limited flat land along the rivers, these trails became the foundation for many of the state's roads and remain so to this day. For instance, Route 322 along the Juniata River in Mifflin County has to follow the Indian path as high mountains make this the only sensible entrance to the county from the south. The colony of Pennsylvania began buildings roads as early as 1686, and beginning in 1700, King's Highways were opened linking Philadelphia to Morristown, Chester, and Easton. The great Conestoga Road—named after the wagons made in Lancaster and elsewhere that carried settlers westward and goods in both directions—opened in 1741 from Philadelphia to Lancaster. General Forbes' troops hacked out the road to Pittsburgh in 1758 that still bears his name—in the city itself, it continues as Forbes Avenue. The first paved road in the United States outside a city connected Philadelphia and Lancaster. Built between 1792 and 1794, it was built by the Philadelphia and Lancaster Turnpike Company, ran sixty-five miles, and cost nearly a half-million dollars. Despite nine toll points, it still reduced transportation costs by two-thirds. Turnpikes operated by private companies that charged tolls soon covered the state, but their pavements (stone with gravel on top) greatly reduced the time of travel and overall costs. The National Road, begun in 1806 and the only highway funded by the federal government in this era, connected Cumberland, Maryland, with Illinois, and passed through Uniontown and Washington, Pennsylvania. By 1830, Pennsylvania had over 3,000 miles of roads, operated by over 200 turnpike companies chartered by the state legislature.

Before the age of steam, water travel was much more efficient than land. Durham boats, invented about 1750 by iron works owner Robert Durham, were barges up to forty feet long that could be rowed or pulled along shore in only twenty inches of water. They plied the Delaware, Schuylkill and Susquehanna Rivers and ferried Washington across the Delaware to fight the battle of Trenton. Keelboats from western Pennsylvania floated 1,500 miles down the Ohio River from Pittsburgh to New Orleans beginning in the 1790s. Their tough crews are still remembered in folklore with the legendary Mike Fink. But rivers could be shallow, dry, or frozen for several months of the years—as they

✧

The First Locomotive, August 8, 1829, Trial Trip of the Stourbridge Lion, *by Clyde Osmer DeLand, c. 1916. The first American locomotive made its run outside Honesdale, Pennsylvania.*
COURTESY OF THE LIBRARY OF CONGRESS.

✧

Above: Roads came first. By 1850,
Pennsylvania was covered with privately
built toll roads. Here is an antique, colored
photograph of the pike near Pittsburgh
outside the town of Pitcairn.
COURTESY OF THE AUTHOR.

Below: Pennsylvania built most of its canals
in the 1820s and 1830s. Here we see canals
in Flemington and the Delaware Canal near
New Hope, Pennsylvania, a charming town
that has numerous restaurants, shops, the
Bucks County Playhouse, and still offers
mule rides down the canal. Many canal
towpaths, like that of the Delaware, are now
scenic walkways.
COURTESY OF THE AUTHOR.

were in the cold nineteenth century—and contain rapids, or underwater shoals and snags. In 1797, the Conewago Canal, the state's first, opened along the Susquehanna in York County. Although only a mile and a quarter long, it made the river navigable to Baltimore by circumventing the Conewago Falls.

The Union Canal Company, formed in 1811, foreshadowed a network that soon extended throughout the state. Most spectacular was the Main Line Canal Company, built by the state, founded in 1828 in response to New York's Erie Canal completed three years before. It connected Philadelphia with Pittsburgh. After roads and then a rail line brought goods to the Susquehanna, canals conveyed them on boats to the forty-mile Allegheny Portage Railroad that carried them up and down inclined planes over

several mountain ridges before they resumed their water journey. Pennsylvania companies ultimately built 853 miles of canals. Many canals had numerous locks; the Lehigh Canal turned that river into a series of over sixty dams and locks from White Haven to Easton on the Delaware. Built in the 1820s largely to transport coal on barges, it was destroyed in a flood in 1862.

John Fitch invented the world's first steamboat in Pennsylvania in 1787, but does not receive the credit for it. His vessel ran for three years from Philadelphia to Burlington, New Jersey and was observed by members of the Constitutional Convention. Lancaster, Pennsylvania native Robert Fulton is more commonly regarded as the inventor, since his ship *Clermont* led to service that continues to this day. Regular service in Pennsylvania only began on the Ohio to the Mississippi in 1813, and from Philadelphia to Baltimore and New York in the 1820s.

By the Civil War, however, railroads had come to dominate Pennsylvania's landscape and trade. The state contained several of the nation's great lines—the Erie in the northern part of the state, the Baltimore and Ohio in the southeast, and the Reading connecting Philadelphia and the coal regions. Greatest of all was the Pennsylvania Railroad, which by 1871 connected Philadelphia, New York, and Baltimore with Pittsburgh, Chicago, St. Louis, and points in between. Under the direction of J. Edgar Thompson and Tom Scott, whose protégé was Andrew Carnegie, it became the largest corporation and the biggest freight carrier in the world by 1900. Majestic turn-of-the-century Pennsylvania Stations still stand in Baltimore and Philadelphia (New York tore down the grandest one in 1963). Most of the nation's coal, iron, and steel were transported on its tracks. Scott was a political power, too—in 1876 he brokered the deal between the Republican and Democratic parties in Washington, D.C. that gave the disputed presidential election to Rutherford B. Hayes in return for patronage and internal improvements for the South.

Giving large businesses like Carnegie Steel and Standard Oil rebates and capable of getting anything it wanted from the Pennsylvania legislature, the Pennsylvania figured prominently in the great strike of 1877. Cutting jobs and wages during a national depression and compelling

workers to operate more dangerous double-engine trains, the strike spread to the nation's rail lines. As the state militias tried to force the lines open, it fired into crowds, killing twenty and wounding seventy people in Pittsburgh alone. President Hayes, acting at the behest of the corporation that had made him president, decided to send in federal troops to run the trains on the grounds the Constitution required the government to deliver the mail, and thereby ended the strike. This was the first time the national government used federal troops in a labor dispute. Armories resembling medieval fortresses were built in major cities where citizens threatened by labor unrest could retreat and arm themselves if necessary.

The Pennsylvania and its fellow railroads flourished until the 1950s, when the federally subsidized Interstate Highway System and cheap oil led to an increase in automobile and truck traffic and a decline in both passenger and freight railroads. After merging with the New York Central in 1958, the Penn Central declared bankruptcy in 1970 in the largest business failure in American history. Today, many railroad tracks, like canal tow paths, provide pleasant walkways and bikeways.

Pennsylvania had already anticipated the interstates of today by constructing the Pennsylvania Turnpike, the nation's first limited access super-highway, which was started in 1937 with federal New Deal funding and opened in 1940 with over half of its present 327 miles completed. Today, it is maintained and improved entirely by motorists' tolls.

Pennsylvania railroads, however, did more than provide the sinews that enabled Pennsylvania to become America's leading industrial state (New York's wealth was built on international trade.) They enabled the Union to supply and transfer its forces with ease during the Civil War. And it was the crucial rail junction of Harrisburg—where lines running north to south crossed those running east to west—that was the object of Robert E. Lee's march into Pennsylvania that ended with the Battle of Gettysburg and changed the course of history.

✧

Above: The River Boat *Ruby Glassner Shilliday, 1937, Pittsburgh. 31.5" x 44" oil on canvas. An example of the steamboats that plied the waters of Pennsylvania in the nineteenth century.*

NO. 90. COURTESY OF THE EDWARD STEIDLE MUSEUM, COLLEGE OF EARTH AND MINERAL SCIENCE, PENN STATE UNIVERSITY.

Below: Train yards outside Reading, as they appeared about 1900. The Reading, the Pennsylvania, the Erie, and the Baltimore and Ohio were the greatest of the lines that crisscrossed the state during most of the 19th and 20th centuries.

COURTESY OF THE AUTHOR.

THE CIVIL WAR

There is no battlefield in the United States like Gettysburg. Dozens of monuments, erected by states, regiments, or through voluntary subscriptions dot the countryside. (The Confederate ones tend to be in better shape, as they were not allowed until the 1900s.) The town itself, realizing the tremendous potential for economic growth through tourism, promoted battlefield tours and visits to nearby springs almost as soon as the Civil War ended. Every July, Gettysburg is the site of the world's largest battlefield reenactment. Museums abound in the town and surrounding areas. President Dwight Eisenhower chose to spend his final years there on a farm.

The attention is justified. Had General Lee defeated the union army in a three-day battle that claimed over fifty thousand lives, resistance all over the North to a draft that began on July 4, 1863, the day after the battle ended, would have broken out into open rebellion and the Union soldiers rushed from Gettysburg to New York City to put down the worst riots could not have been mobilized. Gettysburg may not have defeated the South, but along with the surrender of Vicksburg to General Grant on July 4 that gave the North control of the Mississippi River, it marked the beginning of the end.

Besides taking place on Pennsylvania soil, the victory at Gettysburg was directed by Philadelphian George Gordon Meade, the second native of that city to command the North's largest force, the Army of the Potomac. The first, George McClellan, who had twice failed to defeat the Confederates, still managed to poll 45 percent of the popular vote when he ran for President as the Democratic peace candidate against Abraham Lincoln in 1864. Winfield Scott Hancock, another Pennsylvania Democrat who ran unsuccessfully for president in 1880, commanded the army's second corps at Gettysburg.

Pennsylvania's critical role in winning the Civil War extended far beyond Gettysburg. Even before Fort Sumter, in December, 1860, a crowd in Pittsburgh foiled Virginia native Secretary of War William Floyd's order that guns from the local arsenal be shipped South for the impending conflict. When the war began in April, 1861, Governor Andrew Curtin rushed Pennsylvania's "First Defenders" to Washington to protect a federal government surrounded by hostile slave-owning territory in Maryland and Virginia. Nicholas Biddle, a black volunteer from Pottsville, was the war's first casualty when a southern sympathizer in Baltimore threw a brick at his head and wounded him. (Historians usually note that the Fifty-Fourth Massachusetts supplied the North's first black troops, but small numbers of African Americans, like Biddle, served without fanfare in integrated units in some communities.) Curtin was also instrumental in bringing the nation's Republican governors together at Altoona in 1862 before the mid-term Congressional elections to issue a strong statement of support for the war effort. Known as the soldiers' friend, Curtin worked hard to ensure the troops were properly cared for when they were discharged or wounded.

During the Civil War era, more Pennsylvanians were nationally prominent figures than at any time since. President James Buchanan, Democrat of Lancaster, who served from 1857 to 1861, tried unsuccessfully to avert the war by favoring the South. Pennsylvania responded not only by voting for Lincoln, but by remaining the most staunchly Republican state in the nation until the 1930s. Republican Congressman David Wilmot of Towanda had proposed in 1846 that no slave territory be added to the nation as a result of the Mexican War, a measure adopted by the House of Representatives although not by the Senate or President. Congressman Thaddeus Stevens of Lancaster led the "Radical Republicans" who unsuccess-

fully urged that Southern Confederates be deprived of their citizenship and property and that Southern blacks be rewarded for supporting the Union with their lands, farm animals, and supplies. Living with a mixed race woman, Stevens insisted on being buried in a black cemetery, as Lancaster's white ones excluded African Americans. And Jay Cooke, a Philadelphia banker, took a leaf from P. T. Barnum and his circus by organizing rallies, concerts, and parades to advertise war bonds; the North thus avoided the severe inflation the South suffered and was able to pay for most of the war by borrowing money.

Of course, Pennsylvania's railroads and industries contributed mightily to the war effort. The state produced eighty percent of the nation's pig iron, and the Fort Pitt iron works alone turned out fifteen percent of the Union's artillery. Pennsylvania, as the second most populous state, was second only to New York in supplying soldiers. Women organized associations, culminating in Philadelphia's great Sanitary Fair of 1864, that supplied clothing, medicines, and food to the numerous soldiers who passed through Pennsylvania on their way to the Army of the Potomac. Yet support for the war was not uni-

✛

Another take on Gettysburg: Pickett's Charge, Battle of Gettysburg, July 3, 1863. *About 1930-32. John Kane (1860-1934), artist. Watercolor and gouache on paper, 14.5" × 23.5". Kane offers another perspective on this great battle, showing the action of July 3, when the Confederate army lost 7,500 of nearly 15,000 men in a head-on attack on the Union line.*

KITCHEN — DINING ROOM — LAUNDRY

OFFICERS DINING ROOM — LADIES KITCHEN

BATH ROOM — WASH ROOM

CORNER OF BROAD ST. & PHILADELPHIA. WASHINGTON AVENUE. CITIZENS VOLUNTEER HOSPITAL

STORE ROOM — INTERIOR OF HOSPITAL — DRUG ROOM

✧

The huge Citizen Volunteer Hospital, located at the corner of Broad St. and Washington Ave. in Philadelphia, built entirely by private funds, typifies support for the Union war effort on the part of many citizens and suggests the huge numbers of casualties. Lithograph by James Queen.

versal: the Molly Maguires, Irish immigrants who worked in the coal mines of northeastern Pennsylvania, resisted the draft and murdered Republicans who supported the war. (The mine owners were therefore able to group union organizers with the terrorist Mollies.) About 2,000 Pennsylvanians fought for the Confederacy, including General John Pemberton of the old Quaker family, who surrendered to Grant at Vicksburg, and Josiah Gorgas, chief of Confederate Ordnance, who ensured that however hungry or badly clothed they were, Lee's troops always had plenty of ammunition.

Pennsylvania was the only non-slave state invaded by Confederate troops. Besides Gettysburg, Confederate raiders twice attacked the city of Chambersburg, in 1862 and 1864, burning it the second time when its citizens could not produce $50,000 in gold.

Southern complaints about the burning of Atlanta ring hollow if we remember that Confederate forces had done the same to Chambersburg, and without the excuse that it was a leading industrial center.

The main effect of the Civil War on Pennsylvania was economic. Steel, oil, iron, textile, and railroad industries and financial institutions made large profits and strongly identified their interests with the Republican party that gave them high tariffs to protect them from British competition. The politicians and businesses were linked by colorful and corrupt bosses, of whom Simon Cameron, Lincoln's first secretary of war, was the first. The idealism of the Civil War ended, and the Gilded Age began, where those called industrial statesmen by some and robber barons by others dominated Pennsylvania, and America, until the 1930s.

Kiers Rock Oil. Gould, artist.

Early oil refining.

NO. 151. COURTESY OFTHE EDWARD STEIDLE MUSEUM,
COLLEGE OF EARTH AND MINERAL SCIENCE, PENN
STATE UNIVERSITY.

PENNSYLVANIA INDUSTRY:
IRON, OIL AND LUMBER

"Valley Forge" is famous as the campsite of the American army during the Revolutionary War. But its name gives a clue to its other significance—it was one of more than eighty furnaces (which made the iron pigs into rods, straps, and plates) or forges (where these were finished into products) that were producing one-seventh of the western world's iron in Pennsylvania by 1776. (Another 83 were built by 1800.) Beginning in 1716 with Thomas Rutter's Coventry Iron Works on Manatawny Creek near Pottstown, iron was Pennsylvania's first great industry aside from milling grain. The British Iron Act of 1750 encouraged Americans to ship raw iron to England, and they responded by increasing their exports from 3,000 to 8,000 tons annually in the next quarter-century. They also responded by ignoring the provision in the law which forbade finishing the iron or erecting new slitting mills or tool manufactories. Had they not done so, the state would not have supplied many of the rifles, cannons, and bullets that won the Revolution.

An iron furnace or forge was called a "plantation," and it was a large-scale enterprise, as the museum towns Hopewell Furnace in Berks County and Curtin Village in Centre County illustrate. Iron was manufactured in rural areas where it was found. Acres of timber were required to heat and forge the iron, which was readily available near the surface throughout much of Pennsylvania. Water powered the furnace—as of 1850 over half the furnaces in the state had not yet switched to steam. Some furnaces used slave labor but most relied on permanent white crews or hired free labor. To a large extent, furnaces were self-sufficient communities that grew their own food and made their own tools.

Before the Civil War, Pennsylvania's iron industry, centered in the Lehigh Valley, produced over half of the half million tons of iron—most of it used for the rails of the nation's rapidly expanding railroad network—in the United States. By the 1860s, the introduction of coal and charcoal and rail transport led to the rise of iron factories in cities such as Pittsburgh, Scranton, and Johnstown. In the years after the Civil War Andrew Carnegie set the precedent where steel companies would make their own iron: when Carnegie sold his business and US Steel was founded in 1901, it controlled 60 percent of the iron it used for making two-thirds of the steel in the United States. Yet independent Pennsylvania iron manufacturers did not go out of business; they made specialized high-quality products, used largely skilled union labor—the Sons of Vulcan, founded in Pittsburgh in 1861, became the Amalgamated Association of Iron and Steel Workers in 1876—and continued to flourish until the Great Depression.

Before Edwin L. Drake struck oil on August 27, 1859 after drilling a well seventy feet deep at Titusville in northwestern Pennsylvania, whales and oil that rose to the surface had been the principal source of a product used primarily for kerosene lamps. Drake invented but failed to patent the drive pipe, divided into sections ten feet long and six inches wide that could be driven through rock by manpower, as well as animals and steam. Almost immediately, the boom along Oil Creek resembled the California Gold Rush. Towns sprang up overnight and became ghost towns when the wells ran dry: Pithole City, founded in 1865, boasted 15,000 people and fifty hotels within three months and went out of existence in January, 1866. Speculators, mostly in Philadelphia, bought up land at a furious pace, and paid constantly increasing prices in the hope of striking it rich. The landscape, its trees cut down, became a barren

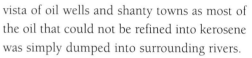

1859 THE OLD DRAKE OIL-WELL. 1859.

vista of oil wells and shanty towns as most of the oil that could not be refined into kerosene was simply dumped into surrounding rivers.

Given its remote location, Pennsylvania oil was at first shipped by wagons on dirt roads that locals called "almost impassable, scarcely jackassable" or by flatboats down the Allegheny River to Pittsburgh. In 1865, John D. Rockefeller of Cleveland, a wealthy produce merchant, began to obtain his near monopoly of the fields in Pennsylvania and eastern Ohio through vertical integration—owning everything needed to convert oil into kerosene, including oil wells, wagons, refineries, and barrels. But his greatest coups were the deals he made with the New York Central, Erie, and Pennsylvania Railroads that soon handled most of the traffic. Given the volume he could supply, he arranged to send all his oil on these lines at half the price they charged his competitors and even received a rebate on oil his competitors shipped. When Tom Scott of the Pennsylvania Railroad deserted Rockefeller for the independent Petroleum Producers Union, Rockefeller countered by building refineries in New Jersey to corner the export market, bought up the most lucrative pipelines that were coming into use, undersold his competitors until they sold out or went broke, and rented all the available tanks and railroad cars even if he didn't use them. While independents continued to compete,

Petroleum Refinery, *Christian Jacob Walter, artist. Before 1935. Bradford. 24" X 32". Oil on canvas.*

NO. 63. COURTESY OF THE EDWARD STEIDLE MUSEUM, COLLEGE OF EARTH AND MINERAL SCIENCE, PENN STATE UNIVERSITY.

by 1878 Rockefeller's Company, Standard Oil, controlled 97 percent of the refineries in the country and dominated the industry until in 1911 the Supreme Court broke his monopoly under the Sherman Anti-Trust Act of 1887 that outlawed "combinations in restraint of trade." Rockefeller, for his part, although most of his wealth came from Pennsylvania, lived in Cleveland and New York. A strict Baptist, he gave away over half of his fortune of nearly one billion dollars (he was one of the world's wealthiest men) to the Rockefeller Medical Institute and Baptist educational endeavors, including southern black colleges, before his death at the age of 98 in 1937.

Pennsylvania's oil was used mostly for kerosene; by the time Henry Ford began turning out automobiles in great numbers after 1897, Pennsylvania's fields were almost exhausted, and oil had been discovered in Texas and Oklahoma. Yet there still may be oil deep below Pennsylvania's surface, and if prices rise high enough it may become profitable to pump it. As of 1980, only Texas refined more oil than Pennsylvania.

Pennsylvania was also the nation's leader in producing timber in the 1860s; it ranked second in 1870 and fourth in 1900. Nearly every tree in contemporary Pennsylvania is either second (or later) growth; a small stand of the magnificent trees that filled the state may still be viewed at Alan Seeger State Park in Centre County. The lumber industry resembled the oil in its primitive, crime-ridden, and overwhelmingly male camps. Sawed into eight to twenty foot logs, timber was taken to the nearest river and floated downstream to sawmills. Williamsport was the lumber capital of the world from the 1860s to 1880s, and the Susquehanna was sometimes so choked with logs that they could not move. Men such as Frederick Weyerhaueser and William Dodge were among the lumber barons; many of them lived on "millionaires' row" or South Fourth Street in Williamsport, an elegant street that has been restored to much of its former glory. It was only appropriate that Pennsylvania's Gifford Pinchot, whose father and grandfather had made much of their fortune selling lumber from northeastern Pennsylvania, became the founder of scientific forestry in America. Today, numerous state parks and protected streams ensure that the state's natural beauties, which have restored themselves in large measure after the late nineteenth century oil and lumber booms, will not suffer a similar fate again.

COAL AND THE ANTHRACITE REGION

❖

Anthracite Colliery in its Mountain Setting.
View of a typical anthracite coal mine:
colliery is in front, town in the middle,
mountains surround.

COURTESY OF THE AUTHOR.

There are two sorts of coal. Hard or anthracite is found mostly deep below ground, is tough to burn, difficult to extinguish, and burns clean. Bituminous or soft is found near the surface, burns easily, produces lots of smoke, and is easier to put out. Nearly all America's anthracite coal, some 22 billion estimated tons, was found in northeastern Pennsylvania in Schuylkill, Luzerne, Lackawanna, and Carbon counties. Bituminous coal deposits once underlaid the whole western third of the state and extended southward to Alabama: Pennsylvania's share alone amounted to 75 billion tons. Coal was the foundation of Pennsylvania's industrial might. Its major canals and railroads were built to haul anthracite, which was used to heat homes and propel furnaces. Bituminous coal could be converted into coke and used with iron to manufacture steel.

Anthracite coal was discovered as early as the 1750s, when an Indian brought it to Nazareth to assist a gunsmith whose furnace ran out of wood, and it was used to heat forts and forge cannons and guns in both the French and Indian War and American Revolution. But the origin of Pennsylvania's role as the world's leading producer of anthracite coal is linked to the story of Philip Ginter. It appears that Ginter first arrived in Philadelphia in 1746 with a boatload of other German immigrants. He then settled in Berks County, where he experienced tragedy during the Seven Years' War. Indians scalped his wife and captured three of his children. His "discovery" of the first anthracite in the great eastern coal field of Pennsylvania remains one of those historical episodes that lies somewhere between fact and folklore. Although local tradition paints him as a poor hunter, in fact he was a prominent local businessman, a miller who served as a church trustee, and a road commissioner. Ginter had been looking for anthracite for a few years before he "stumbled" onto it in 1791. Seven years earlier, the Pennsylvania legislature had identified the shipment of coal to Philadelphia as one of the reasons the Schuylkill River needed to be made more navigable in its northern course.

Appreciation of anthracite's value outside the military sphere was slow. In 1792, Colonel Jacob Weiss, Charles Cist and others formed the Lehigh Coal Mine Company. Although unprofitable for them, Jacob Cist (Charles' son and nephew of Colonel Weiss) and his partners took over the 10,000 company's acres and did their best to transport and market the abundant coal to Philadelphians. One major step in raising public interest in coal occurred in 1808, when Judge Jesse Fell of Wilkes-Barre substituted anthracite for wood in his home fireplace and found it cheaper and cleaner. Interest grew, but not sufficiently, until the area Ginter discovered was leased to Josiah White and Erskine Hazard in 1818. They formed the giant Lehigh Coal and Navigation Company and developed a cost-efficient canal route to market. The discovery of coal was not enough; large quantities had to be carried to cities via water for it to be profitable. By the Civil War, the largest coal companies were in fact operated by railroads that provided access to the fields. The Philadelphia and Reading Railroad, led by two of the most notorious business leaders in American history, Frank Gowen (who busted the anthracite union by linking them to the Molly Maguires in 1877) and later George Baer (who refused to negotiate with miners in the 1902 coal strike until President Theodore Roosevelt forced him to) attempted without success to dominate the industry.

Coal proved profitable for the entrepreneurial and management class; for the poor folk who worked the mines, it offered subsistence wages and a high rate of industrial accidents. Until the 1870s, most mineworkers were Scots and Irish who were supervised by English bosses. Later, the Irish and Scots moved up to direct the immigrants from Poland, Slovakia, the Ukraine, Italy, and Hungary who took their places. Frequently the whole family worked: men beginning in their teenaged years worked in the mines, chopping coal out of rock—sometimes gunpowder was used first to give them access—and putting it in carts pulled by horses and mules. Then it was sent to the breakers, large buildings where young boys separated coal from rock as it tumbled down chutes. Women took in boarders to make ends meet, and by the early twentieth century young girls worked in textile factories.

Work was dangerous: mine cave-ins, gas explosions, fires, floods and injuries to arms and legs were frequent. Long-term diseases such as emphysema and "black lung" were not even named in the mid-nineteenth century, but shortened lives that were spent in large part underground.

Many miners lived in patch towns near the coal fields, owned by coal companies, where they rented houses and shopped at company stores. These rural towns tended to be drab and without sidewalks, sewage, or sanitation.

The immigrants formed their own associations to make life more bearable. Churches, Roman Catholic or Orthodox, were frequently formed by people of a particularly nationality—there might be several Catholic churches in a small town. Weddings and funerals were elaborate and expensive displays of joy and grief. Since the coal companies provided little relief for the disabled or families of the deceased, immigrants formed insurance societies which in effect functioned as banks. The rich culture of the region appears in the persistence of festivals and ethnic loyalties in the region's towns to this day.

Mine owners used industrial spies and played ethnic groups against each other to discourage unionization, but the United Mine Workers became entrenched after great struggles. First they were tarnished by association with the Molly Maguires, a terrorist organization that opposed the draft and the Civil War by murdering prominent Republicans. In 1877, twenty leaders were hung following investigations by Pinkerton detectives and prosecution by company lawyers. They may or may not have been guilty; nearly all the evidence was supplied by a Pinkerton detective who had successfully infiltrated the group.

✧

The Miners (The Old Mine Mule).
Richard Harrison Crist, artist. 1934.
Monongahela, Pennsylvania. 30" × 36",
oil on canvas.

NO. 10. COURTESY OF THE EDWARD STEIDLE MUSEUM, COLLEGE OF EARTH AND MINERAL SCIENCE, PENN STATE UNIVERSITY.

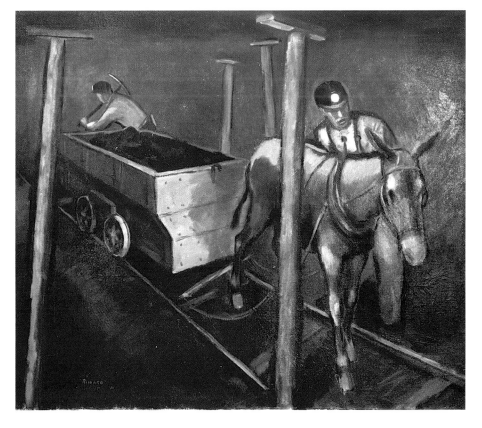

Pennsylvania was the only state in America that permitted private companies to organize local police forces. The Mollies were investigated, arrested, and prosecuted (the district attorney was also a lawyer for the mine companies) by the mine owners. All the state supplied was the courtroom, jail, and rope for the hangings. But after the 1897 Lattimer Massacre, in which nineteen peaceful miners carrying American flags were fired on by coal and local police forces, sympathy for the coal

unions grew. John Mitchell and William Wilson, who had both risen through the ranks in the mines, led a 1902 walkout by 150,000 workers that marked the first attempt by the United States government to mediate rather than put down a strike. Denouncing the conditions under which miners worked, President Theodore Roosevelt secured a ten percent wage hike for the workers. Wilson, a miner from Blossburg, Pennsylvania with an eighth-grade education, became the first secretary of labor under President Woodrow Wilson (no relation) in 1913.

Although coal production in the anthracite has declined since the mid-twentieth century, some companies still mine profitably and, if the price of oil continues to rise, may well begin to secure energy from culm, the huge heaps of refuse removed from the anthracite. The Lehigh Coal and Navigation Company lasted until 1965, when it was bought out by Bethlehem Steel. At its peak in 1919, it employed 11,000 people and produced five million tons of coal. In 1989, the company was reincorporated under its original name and continues to function. Yet the total number of coal miners in the state, peaking at over 300,000 before World War I, was under 25,000 by the 1990s. While mechanization accounts for some of the loss, most remaining bituminous coal is too dirty, and the anthracite too far underground to be mined profitably.

✧

Pittsburgh at Night. *Betty Rendleman,*

artist. Before 1937. 16" × 24". Oil on canvas.

NO. 13. COURTESY OF THE EDWARD STEIDLE MUSEUM,
COLLEGE OF EARTH AND MINERAL SCIENCE, PENN
STATE UNIVERSITY.

STEEL, CARNEGIE, AND PITTSBURGH

Although steel is associated with the Pittsburgh region and Andrew Carnegie, it flourished first in eastern Pennsylvania. Rebecca Lukens, America's first woman industrialist, saved Lukens Steel after the early death of her husband in 1829; it survived into the 21st century and produced steel for the nation's first nuclear powered submarine, the World Trade Center, and the St. Louis Arch. Bethlehem Steel was second in size only to Carnegie and US Steel. Its president in the late nineteenth century, Charles Schwab, built one of the most elegant mansions in New York City. Until the 1870s, iron rather than steel was the dominant metal produced in America—the Civil War was fought with iron—but then the steel industry benefited enormously from two technological innovations. The Bessemer Process, which became widely used in the 1870s, blew cold air through iron. The open-hearth process enabled huge quantities of steel to be forged in a furnace.

Andrew Carnegie came to dominate the American steel industry. Born in poverty in Scotland in 1835, he came to America at the age of thirteen. He worked as a bobbin boy, a telegraph operator, and a supervisor at the Pennsylvania Railroad. After the Civil War, he entered the iron industry before constructing the Thomson Steel Mill in 1873 that used the new Bessemer process. It was named after the president of the Pennsylvania Railroad and Carnegie's mentor. The Pennsylvania soon became Carnegie's best customer.

Carnegie owed his success to controlling his key materials and employing able men. He owned and purchased the best ore from Lake Superior; he made Henry Clay Frick, who was the nation's largest manufacturer of the coke essential for steel production, his executive officer. In 1901, he sold his holdings to J. P. Morgan for $350 million. Carnegie Steel became the largest of the ten steel companies that formed US Steel, which then replaced the Pennsylvania Railroad as the largest corporation in the world. By 1910, Pennsylvania was producing sixty percent of the ten million tons of steel in the United States. The state alone out-produced any other country on earth.

Carnegie was also the nation's most visible and outspoken philanthropist. In his book *The Gospel of Wealth*, Carnegie argued that "he who dies rich dies disgraced". In his lifetime, he gave away over $350 million dollars (worth uncountable billions in today's terms). His most famous gifts were to construct over 2,000 Carnegie libraries. He also provided funding for the first privately financed building at Penn State, Carnegie Hall in New York, and the Carnegie Institute in Pittsburgh (now Carnegie-Mellon University).

Yet on the other hand, Carnegie believed that if he failed to manage his plants as efficiently as possible, someone else would do so and put him out of business. (The Communist thinker Karl

Marx, by the way, agreed with this judgment, stating the capitalist was as much a victim of economic forces as the worker.) Carnegie steel workers labored six days a week, and every other week did a twenty-four hour shift. Boarding houses would rent out the same bed to two men who worked alternate shifts. In 1889, Carnegie had negotiated a settlement at his Homestead plant with the Amalgamated United Steel, Iron, and Tin Workers, but then declared that when the three-year contract expired he would no longer recognize the union. When the workers struck, Carnegie was out of the country, vacationing in the Scottish countryside he loved and where he had been born. Henry Clay Frick did not hesitate to call in the Pinkerton detectives, who approached the Works by water and tried to storm them before surrendering to the strikers. Three Pinkertons and seven strikers were killed before Governor John Pattison called in 8,000 state militamen to restore order. During the strike, anarchist Alexander Berkman wounded Frick in an attempt to assassinate him. After five months on strike, the Homestead Works reopened; three-fifths of the workers were either fired or left. The Homestead Strike also caused a falling-out between Carnegie and Frick. Carnegie claimed

to have no knowledge of what Frick was up to, and criticized him for measures of which he himself approved.

Unionization did not come to most of western Pennsylvania until the 1930s. The American Federation of Labor (AFL), which in 1886 succeeded the Federation of Organized Trade and Labor Unions, after the Homestead Strike abandoned the unskilled workers who formed the great majority of steelworkers. New Deal legislation permitted union organizers to do their work and hold elections under federal protection, leading to sit-down strikes (that prevented non-union workers from entering the plants and doing the work), at steel mills throughout western Pennsylvania, and the creation of the Congress of Industrial Organizations (CIO) which held its first convention at Pittsburgh in 1938. Pittsburgh's Philip Murray was its President from 1940 to 1958, although its founding was most symbolized by the fiery John L. Lewis.

Besides union agreements, state and federal laws regulating conditions and hours of labor made life better for steelworkers during the twentieth century. Second and third generation steel workers moved up from the unskilled jobs immigrants held. Immigration was usually a family affair: young men and women were sent over alone and expected to scrimp and save in order to bring over other family members. In many cases this worked, but forty percent of all immigrants returned to their country of origin, disillusioned by working conditions and the absence of social and family life to soften it.

The great works at Homestead, Clarion, Duquesne, and McKeesport are no longer open. Until the 1960s, Pennsylvania steel was prospering, but beginning in the 1970s, the United States began importing steel from Brazil, Korea, and other countries with newer equipment and workers who, like Americans a hundred years ago, were willing to toil long hours merely to survive. Employment in the steel industry fell from 150,000 to 50,000 between 1974 and 1991. The destruction of the great furnaces signaled that Pennsylvania, like the United States, could no longer rely on heavy industry to underwrite its prosperity.

✧

Tapping an Electric Arc (Steel) Furnace.
Ralph D Dunkelberger, Reading 1936.

30" × 36" oil on canvas.

NO. 31. COURTESY OF THE EDWARD STEIDLE MUSEUM, COLLEGE OF EARTH AND MINERAL SCIENCE, PENN STATE UNIVERSITY.

Glass Blowers, *Charles F. Ulrich, artist.*
NO. 321. COURTESY OF THE EDWARD STEIDLE MUSEUM, COLLEGE OF EARTH AND MINERAL SCIENCE PENN STATE UNIVERSITY.

FROM BEER TO BUGGIES: PENNSYLVANIA'S INDUSTRIAL GREATNESS

Ever since William Rittenhouse opened the first paper mill in America in 1690 on Wissahickon Creek, a few miles north of Philadelphia at the time (Rittenhouse Town is preserved as a museum village), Pennsylvania businesses have provided numerous products locally, to the nation, and to the world. For instance, we owe the windproof "Zippo" lighter to George Blaisdell, who opened his plant in Bradford, Pennsylvania, in 1932 in the middle of the Great Depression. Since then, the factory has manufactured over four hundred million of these products, each guaranteed to last a lifetime. The first steel six-foot tape measure was also developed at the Bradford site. Other Pennsylvania inventions include: the first Ferris wheel, invented by George Washington Ferris of Pittsburgh, who introduced his invention at the Columbian Exposition in Chicago in 1893, and the first piece of bubble gum, invented by Walter Diemer in 1928 and manufactured by the Fleer Corporation for which he worked in Philadelphia.

Pennsylvania boasts America's oldest brewery, founded in Pottsville by Frederick Yuengling in 1829 as the Eagle Brewery, and operating continuously on its current site since 1831. Still a family-run firm, Yuengling has opened new plants in Tampa, Florida, and St. Clair, Pennsylvania since the 1990s, but maintains the original plant, which also offers tours and a museum. Surviving Prohibition by constructing a dairy that manufactured ice cream, Yuengling celebrated the end of the dry years by sending a case of beer to President Franklin Roosevelt.

Beer was being manufactured in Pennsylvania as early as 1795, when it was first brewed commercially in Pittsburgh, the numerous hills and caves in the vicinity serving as excellent places to keep the beverage cool and stored. Hard cider, however, was the principal beverage favored until the mid-nineteenth century. Apples and sugar were all people needed to brew their own, and at up to fifteen percent alcohol, it packed a wallop contemporary ciders cannot approach. But as German immigrants began to arrive in large numbers in the 1820s, they brought with them their taste for beer, as well as brewing techniques.

Despite Yuengling's continued success, the most famous Pennsylvania producer is the Iron City Brewing Company, founded in 1861 by Edward Frauenstein, who began brewing the beer of that name still sold today. Within five years he had built the factory at Liberty Avenue and 34 Street that remains the company's headquarters. In 1899, Iron City merged with twenty others to form the Pittsburgh Brewing Company, the largest in Pennsylvania and the third largest in the nation. It survived Prohibition (1919-1933) by producing soft drinks and "near beer," and also weathered a post-World War II consolidation that left only forty breweries in the United States. Working with Alcoa Aluminum—also headquartered in Pittsburgh—Pittsburgh Beer produced the first snap-top can in 1962, the first resealable twist-off top the following year, and the first light beer (Mark V) in 1976. Today, numerous microbreweries flourish in Pennsylvania, the longest-lived being Straub's, brewed first in Pittsburgh in 1831, then

as part of Eberhart and Ober, (which became part of the Pittsburgh Brewing Company), and finally on its own in St. Mary's.

Hershey, Pennsylvania, is the site of the world's largest chocolate and cocoa manufacturing plant. Begun in 1894 as the Hershey Chocolate Company, located in the midst of the rich dairy farms of Lancaster, Dauphin, and Lebanon counties, in 1900 it produced the first Hershey Bar. Milton Hershey, its founder, built a town around the factory that bears his name. A lover of children who had none of his own, Hershey donated his fortune to the Milton S. Hershey School for orphan boys and lavished public gardens and an amusement park on his town where adults too can experience the process of chocolate-making in a delightful setting. The Hershey Hotel is in Spanish-American style, as Hershey visited Cuba where he purchased the sugar fields needed for his factory and fell in love with the architecture.

Early Pennsylvania was also a center of the auto industry, although manufacturing quickly moved to the Detroit area. Over fifty firms turned out trucks and cars in southeastern Pennsylvania between 1900 and 1920, notably that of Charles Duryea, who had launched the first gas-driven automobile in the United States in Springfield, Massachusetts in 1895. Duryea moved his operations to Reading, Pennsylvania in 1900 and to Philadelphia in 1913. But Pennsylvanians built attractive cars modeled on horse buggies, which could not compete in the larger market with Henry Ford's basic, practical Model T. Only the "Fleetwood", a luxury model built to the owner's specifications in the town of that name near Reading, survived after it was sold to Cadillac. But Allentown still produces Mack Trucks, and York the Harley-Davidson motorcycle.

Although Thomas Edison lived in New Jersey, the first building in the world to be "electrified" was the City Hotel in Sunbury, Pennsylvania, on July 4, 1883. Edison himself directed the operation, and the power came from the Edison Illuminating Company Plant at Fourth and Vine Streets. The name most associated with Pennsylvania electricity, however, is George Westinghouse, who successful-

✧
Hotel Edison, Sunbury, first building in the world to use electricity (1883). Installation supervised by Edison himself.

As for the distribution of Pennsylvania's abundant industrial production, no name stands above John Wanamaker. A religious and political reformer, Wanamaker is best known for the department store that until recently bore his name (it is now Lord and Taylor's) opposite City Hall in Philadelphia. Opened by President Taft in 1911, it offered nearly every item needed for the home (except food – though that could be had at a fine restaurant) in an attractive setting where courteous employees waited on customers. Musical concerts centering on an enormous pipe organ further enticed those middle and upper-class people (who could afford the items) to enter the store. Wanamaker is believed to have coined the phrase "the customer is always right" and originated the money-back guarantee with no questions asked. As postmaster general of the United States from 1889 to 1893, he initiated free rural home delivery. But despite his economic achievements, he could not successfully compete in the ruthless realm that was Pennsylvania politics.

ly championed the alternating current invented by Nikolai Tesla as superior to the direct current invented by Edison. Westinghouse had earlier developed the air brake that greatly lessened the number of train wrecks, and discovered the process that converted natural gas into fuel. Employees at his extensive works at Wilmerding, Pennsylvania, near Pittsburgh benefited from an eight-hour day and pension system long before federal rules required them.

Pennsylvania figures in the history of management as well as production. Frederick Winslow Taylor, who did most of his work at Bethlehem Steel in the years around 1900, is generally considered the father of modern scientific management, which for a time was called "Taylorism." His contributions included careful accounting and inventory management; an incentive wage system based on piece work; and systematic planning and use of specialized knowledge. Taylor is sometimes criticized for the ruthlessness with which he subordinated employee welfare to the demands of the company, but modified versions of his theories are now standard practice in modern business.

BOSSES AND PROGRESSIVES

Pennsylvania politics from the Civil War until 1921 was dominated by three men who served in the United States Senate: Simon Cameron, Matthew S. Quay, and Boies Penrose. Known for their corruption in addition to their adroit maneuvering, they made Pennsylvania the most dependably Republican state in the Union. The basis for their power was patronage. As cities grew, streets had to be paved, schools and government buildings erected, gas and electricity provided, and transportation networks laid out. All this meant contracts that could be given to politically favored firms and jobs to the party faithful from construction workers and janitors up to the state's highest officials. Meanwhile, in steel and coal towns, employers lined up their workers, many of whom could not read or speak English, to vote Republican, as did the party leaders in Philadelphia. Speaking from Independence Hall, one boss, bragging about voting lists padded with names of the dead, proclaimed that not only had the Founding Fathers once voted there for independence, but that over a century later many of them continued to vote.

Philadelphia's Democratic party was so weak that the Republicans even gave Democrats a share of the city jobs and paid the rent on the party headquarters to preserve the appearance of a two-party system. Discredited for their partiality to the South, the state's Democrats only elected one governor between the Civil War and 1936, Robert Pattison, who served from 1883 to 1887 and again from 1891 to 1895. With the exception of Progressive Republican Theodore Roosevelt in 1912, Pennsylvania cast its electoral votes for Republicans as well in every election from 1860 to 1932. The Democrats only dominated the state legislature twice, for four years, during that period, and only elected two of seventeen men to serve as United States Senator.

Besides corruption, Pennsylvania Republicans were shrewd enough to remain popular by running Civil War heroes for public office, such as Governors John Geary and James Beaver. Later, ex-professional baseball player John Tener and philanthropist William Sproul gave the party a respectable front: Republican national conventions offered the vice-presidential spot to Beaver in 1880 and Sproul in 1920, but they turned it down. (Presidents James Garfield and Warren Harding, who were chosen in those years, both died: had they accepted, Pennsylvania might have had three presidents instead of only one.)

Simon Cameron engineered the triumph of the Republican machine during the presidential administration of the Democrat James Buchanan (1857-1861), whose Democrats had previously dominated the state's politics. Cameron owed his power to his control of the wealthy Middletown Bank and favors he engineered for the Pennsylvania Railroad, like selling the state's mainline canal system to the railroad in 1857 and securing railroads' exemption from taxes in 1861. The Railroad could also give out favors, including corporate charters the legislature handed it that authorized participation in any form of business including holding stock and owning property in other states. (John D. Rockefeller's Standard Oil was the product of one such charter, and Credit Mobilier, which built the Union Pacific Railroad at an exorbitant cost, was another). Due to Cameron's involvement, Pennsylvania's votes secured for Abraham Lincoln his nomination as the Republican candidate for President in 1860. Promised a cabinet appointment by Lincoln's assistants, he became Secretary of War. Cameron proved hopelessly inept at running a modern war, and was even censored by an overwhelmingly Republican House of Representatives in 1862 for handing out military contracts to political favorites. After a brief stint as Minister to Russia, he returned to the Senate until 1877, when he resigned at age of 78 so the governor of Pennsylvania could appoint his son, J. Donald Cameron, to succeed him as Senator, a post Donald held for another twenty years. On the issues, he staunchly supported a high tariff to protect Pennsylvania's workers and industry from foreign competition and favored harsh punishment of the South for fighting the Civil War.

Unlike his father, Donald Cameron was not a great manager of people. Matthew Quay of Pittsburgh, who had won a Medal of Honor for bravery during the Civil War battle of Fredericksburg, took Simon Cameron's place as the state's Republican boss. Quay's power came from his position as state treasurer, which he used to channel funds into Republican coffers and ensure the party faithful were rewarded with government positions. Elected to the United States Senate in 1887, he served (except for two years following a disputed election in 1901) until his death in 1904. When John Wanamaker ran against him and criticized "Quayism," Quay defeated him and denied any corrupt practice.

Quay's successor, in turn, was Philadelphia's Boies Penrose, "Big Grizzly," a 350-pound giant of a man whose means of controlling Pennsylvania politics made him a nationwide symbol of corruption. A Harvard graduate from a wealthy family who preferred to spend his time in saloons and carousing with politicians—the most famous photograph of him shows him leaving a brothel—his support came from his brother, who owned copper mines, and his willingness to spend $175,000 of his own money each year to grease the political wheels. Matthew Quay recognized his abilities, furthered his career, and in 1897 ensured the state legislature elected him Pennsylvania's junior senator, a position he held until his death in 1921.

Penrose's moments of glory were 1910 and 1920. In 1910, victory for the Democrats seemed certain in the race for governor: four Republicans had been sent to jail through the investigations of the state treasurer, William Berry, who proved they had more than doubled the cost of the new state Capitol and pocketed the difference. Penrose first fixed the Republican convention, nominating a Pittsburgh Congressman and former major league baseball player, John Tener. He then persuaded the Democratic nominee not to accept by promising him a federal judgeship (which President Taft refused), and influenced the delegates not to nominate Berry. Outraged, honest Republicans joined Democrats and ran Berry on a third, the Washington Party, but he split enough votes with the Democrat to ensure Tener a narrow victory. In 1920, Penrose was instrumental in

✧

Above: Simon Cameron.
COURTESY OF THE LIBRARY OF CONGRESS.

Below: Matthew Quay.
COURTESY OF THE LIBRARY OF CONGRESS.

choosing Warren Harding as the Republican nominee for President (he could have had his own Governor Sproul but thought Sproul was too independent-minded) and Andrew Mellon (for whom he personally engineered a change in Pennsylvania's divorce laws to keep his marital woes under wraps) as Secretary of the Treasury.

Penrose was a through and through conservative. He favored business interests and conservative causes unequivocally, opposing the income tax, women's right to vote, pro-labor legislation, and prohibition. The Seventeenth Amendment, which transferred the election of Senators from the state legislatures to the people, was largely passed to defeat him: Penrose amazed his opponents by being an exceptionally popular campaigner who defeated progressive Gifford Pinchot in the 1914 Republican primary and Democratic reform lawyer A. Mitchell Palmer in the general election. Palmer, the future United States Attorney General from 1919 to 1921 who changed his political stripes, instituted the notorious "Red Scare" that imprisoned and deported numerous "Communists."

Notorious for its corruption, Pennsylvania was naturally a principal target of the "muckrakers" and Progressive reformers. Most prominent were Lincoln Steffens, whose book *The Shame of the Cities* branded Philadelphia the worst-run metropolis in the nation: even New

York's boss George Washington Plunkett complained that, unlike New York politicians who may have taken their cut but still provided public services ("honest graft"), the Philadelphians grubbed for every nickel and dime as services and public health deteriorated. Ida Tarbell, who attended Allegheny College in Meadville, focused on Standard Oil as her main target, although to be fair to Rockefeller it should be noted her brother ran a rival oil company and she made up the story that he had cheated a poor widow out of her life savings (she actually ended up with an excellent settlement from Standard Oil).

Pennsylvania reformers were not totally ineffectual, but all too often the laws they passed failed to have the desired effect. Gifford Pinchot, Theodore Roosevelt's Chief of Forestry, had an impeccable reputation but was unable to win the governorship until 1922, the year after Penrose's death. He did so by making a deal with the Mellon interests of Pittsburgh, who dominated Mellon Bank and the Alcoa Aluminum Company, and the Pennsylvania Association of Manufacturers, to oppose the three Vare brothers who ran Philadelphia, who got their start as garbage collectors before becoming the leading city contractors. Pinchot repaid the favor by refusing to certify William Vare's election as United States Senator during a corrupt election in 1926 in which he was Vare's major opponent. Vare responded by throwing Philadelphia's machine votes to a Democrat when Pinchot was re-elected governor in 1930 (by under 50,000 out of over two million votes cast) and opposing Pinchot's efforts to use state funds for public relief during the Depression. The Republican machine continued to govern the state, despite an interlude during the New Deal, until the 1950s. Since then, Pennsylvania has had a competitive two-party system with most successful politicians (Philadelphia's mayor Frank Rizzo and former Republican Senator Rick Santorum being two major, conservative exceptions) being moderates who have to reconcile a very diverse state population.

The most requested image from the Pennsylvania State Archives is Theodore Roosevelt dedicating the current Capitol at Harrisburg in 1906. The white-haired gentleman to his left is Governor Samuel Pennypacker, who later wrote a book exposing the scandals connected with building the edifice.

COURTESY OF THE PENNSYLVANIA STATE ARCHIVES

THE PENNSYLVANIA STATE CAPITOL

When on October 4, 1906, President Theodore Roosevelt dedicated the present Pennsylvania state capitol building, he declared, "It's the handsomest building I ever saw." A century later, after painstaking restoration that began in 1982 and is still in progress, the building still strikes visitors with awe. They gaze upward at the magnificent dome that rises 272 feet and is modeled on the domes of St. Peter's in Rome, or marvel at the marble staircases which resemble the Paris Opera House built by Napoleon III and beautiful legislative chambers. The Capitol is a monument to Pennsylvania's wealth and confidence in its greatness as the twentieth century began.

The State Capitol, which took nine years to build at the cost of $13 million, seems like the bargain of the century. In reality, however, it was the steal of the century. Its architect, the state treasurer, the state auditor general, the superintendent of construction, and the chief contractor were convicted of inflating the real cost of the work by $7.7 million and pocketing the difference. Much of the take came from the culprits' billing the state for every piece of wood, bronze, and paneling either by the foot or by the pound, and then inflating the number of pieces purchased. In addition, brass was passed off as bronze, plaster as mahogany, and chandeliers were weighed down with cheap metals.

Yet this very corruption permitted the Capitol to express Pennsylvania's true history: beneath the state's magnificent surface lay a persistent alternative history not only of corruption and brutality, but of human struggling to achieve a better life and a better world. The very padding of the bills permitted works of art to proliferate throughout the Capitol, filling its nooks and crannies with diverse and fascinating images of Pennsylvania history.

For example, at the top of both the House and the Senate chambers, almost invisible to the legislators on the floor but at a level with the public galleries, are Philadelphia artist William Van Ingen's twenty-four individual stained-glass windows in which women represent "Weaving," "Glass Blowing," "Commerce," and other worthy endeavors such as "Peace," "Education," "Liberty," and "Temperance" (in consumption of alcohol). Yet even from the galleries these noble goals are half-hidden in recessed frames off to the sides. The electorate has to look hard, beyond the various political maneuverings below that threaten to dazzle, to discover the better ideals Pennsylvania has stood for.

Also hidden in nooks, and visible only to those who look upward to see them as they walk through the corridors of power, are fourteen small semi-circular murals (lunettes) also by Van Ingen. Here the religious diversity and importance of Pennsylvania's spiritual heritage may be recovered. Each mural represents a religious group important in the state's history: the Ephrata Cloister, the Moravians, the Dunkards, the Mennonites, and the Quakers are given pride of place over more numerous and mainstream groups like the Catholics and Presbyterians to emphasize Pennsylvania's acceptance of the persecuted.

In contrast, and prominent among the art the Capitol's designers wanted us to focus on, is the work of Edwin Austin Abbey. His thirty-five-foot-wide mural, the *Apotheosis of Pennsylvania*, dominates the House of Representatives Chamber, presenting an imposing, if conventional, view of the state's history. The only woman in the painting is "The Genius of State" (a seated representation of the Goddess of Liberty) and beneath her are arrayed twenty-eight great white men: pioneers, explorers, statesmen, businessmen, scientists, generals, inventors. Closest to ordinary people are two men who made Pennsylvania their home: the radical revolutionary Thomas Paine (an English immigrant who lived in Pennsylvania for seventeen years, moved to Revolutionary France, and died in poverty in New York) and John Fitch (a native of Connecticut who moved to Philadelphia and invented the steamboat twenty-two years before Robert Fulton but failed as a businessman and committed suicide in Kentucky). Paine and Fitch respectively symbolize a commonwealth of people who moved into the state, but also the people who leave Pennsylvaina for lack of opportunity.

Abbey's vision of history also appears in the two murals flanking the *Apotheosis*. On the left, an elegant William Penn surrounded by equally genteel Quakers shakes hands with an Indian warrior of noble bearing, while some of the latter's followers—unlike Penn's who, are standing and looking forward—squat and look backward.

The first state Capitol building at Harrisburg, opened in 1812, burned in 1897. Seen here in Thomas S. Sinclair's lithograph (after Dr. Barr) of View of the Inauguration of Governor James Pollock in Front of the Capitol at Harrisburg, Jan. 16, 1855.

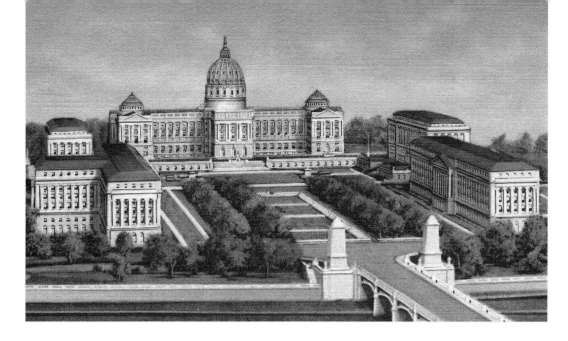

Indians are inferior and backward-looking, lacking in energy, while the erect whites are poised to seize control of the future, albeit peacefully, and tower over them. On the right of the *Apotheosis*, the *Declaration of Independence* is read from a balcony to a group of middle- or upper-class men, while a man with a sword bars a woman with children (who are being signaled to be quiet) from the political arena. Meanwhile, a skeptic scratches his head. The woman and the skeptic cannot make their voices heard in the same space where adult male patriots respond vociferously to the doctrines read to them.

Unlike Abbey, there is no doubt at all about the Violet Oakley murals. Oakley, who finished Abbey's work after his death in 1911, consciously intended to highlight the historical roles of women, minorities, and the poor. Whereas the most notable feature of Abbey's House chamber mural is the female "Genius of State" bearing an oversized sword (ironic for

Pennsylvania, founded as a pacifist haven, although the fact that the sword is upside down is also significant), Oakley, herself a pacifist, directs our eyes in the Senate toward a kneeling woman representing "Unity." She presides over the end of all warfare that so many Americans briefly believed would come with the Allied victory in World War I. Kings give up their crowns, a Red Cross worker joins a soldier in washing the blood off his hands, a black woman cleanses her baby in water to symbolize the end of slavery. Women, one of them pacifist reformer Jane Addams and most of them women of color, join workers in framing a painting from which the wealthy and powerful are absent. Oakley's murals of the Civil War and American Revolution, too, depict soldiers as young men with downcast eyes: in the aftermath of World War I, when she did most of her work, her pacifism indeed reflected a nation determined never to fight again.

Above: The Capitol with the first of many government buildings added as the state's functions increased throughout the twentieth century.

Below: Harrisburg is annually the host of the Pennsylvania State Farm Show. County fairs and 4-H Clubs throughout the state demonstrate that agriculture is still one of the Pennsylvania's most important economic activities in the twenty-first century.

THE GREAT DEPRESSION

Governor Gifford Pinchot breaking ground for one of the many roads built at his urging to combat unemployment and boost the economy during the Great Depression.

COURTESY OF THE PENNSYLVANIA STATE ARCHIVES.

Statistics tell the story: never in American history had anything occurred like the Great Depression that lasted from the Stock Market Crash of 1929 until wartime production to aid the Allies restored economic health in 1940. Pennsylvania's industrial production fell by half from 1929 to 1932, its mineral production from $870 million in 1929 to just over $400 million in 1933. The state turned out fourteen million tons of pig iron in 1929, two million in 1932; seventeen million tons of steel ingots in 1929, three and a half million in 1932. Shantytowns or "Hoovervilles" sprang up outside cities where those who could not pay their rent lived in cardboard boxes or wooden shacks. Unemployment in the state reached 37 percent, 12 points higher than the national average, in 1933 when Franklin Roosevelt was inaugurated President.

Yet such was the strength of the Republican machine that Pennsylvania was the largest state in the union to vote for incumbent Herbert Hoover. Ironically, the man most responsible for the Depression was not Hoover but Pennsylvania's own Andrew Mellon, Secretary of the Treasury from 1921 to 1933. Mellon and a Republican Congress had kept tariffs high, preventing Europeans from selling their products in the United States and thus prevented them from earning enough money to buy American, particularly Pennsylvanian, industrial production. Mellon also insisted European nations pay their war debts from World War I, which contributed to low federal taxes—only paid at the time by the wealthy—but failed to create demand for American products.

Pennsylvania responded to the Depression by electing Progressive Republican Gifford Pinchot as governor in 1930. Pinchot had already served from 1922-1926, and, during his first term, had instituted the Giant Power Survey Board to regulate the state's principal electric utilities. He was also a strong Prohibitionist. When Pennsylvania (which never voted for the measure) refused to provide funds to enforce the federal law, he obtained voluntary contributions from the Women's Christian Temperance Union. Once Prohibition was repealed in 1933, Pinchot did the best he could: Pennsylvania's current liquor laws, with sales restricted to state stores, stem from his refusal in his second term to approve of private sales.

To fight the Depression, Pinchot instituted numerous road-paving projects throughout the state; today Pennsylvania ranks fourth nationwide in its mileage of paved roads. But the conservative legislature, thanks to the vengeful William Vare, even refused to contribute funds to help the unemployed until President Roosevelt threatened to withdraw New Deal funding in 1934. Pinchot proved friendly to organized labor as well, supporting miners who struck the coal industry in western Pennsylvania. Encouraged by his wife Cornelia Bryce Pinchot, who rivaled Eleanor Roosevelt in her support of the unfortunate, he appointed Jews, Catholics, women, and African-Americans to public office. He stood up for academic freedom when state universities tried to remove radical professors.

Pinchot could not succeed himself in 1934: Democrat George Earle defeated the Republican machine candidate. The first Democrat to hold the state house in over seventy years, the liberal Earle won support from the black, immigrant, and working communities: his running mate, Thomas Kennedy, was an official of the United Mine Workers. Despite a conservative State Senate that refused to raise unemployment and medical compensation to workers, he managed to secure a child labor law prohibiting full-time employment for those under sixteen and preventing them from working in dangerous industries. Bills raising milk prices for farmers and prohibiting discrimination in places of public accommodation passed under his regime, but the Republican-controlled Senate denied the state nearly a quarter-billion dollars in federal relief funds for the unemployed by failing to pass bills distributing the money.

Federal programs brought important changes to Pennsylvania even as the state delayed actions. The New Deal Works Progress Administration provided the first $20 million for the Pennsylvania Turnpike; in Philadelphia, the Federal Theater Project put actors and musicians to work performing plays and concerts for free and enriching the cultural lives of the poor and relatively uneducated. The Farm Securities' Administration not only aided farmers economically but created a priceless photographic historical record of rural life that was fading away.

"Gray Towers" (Home of Gifford Pinchot) Milford, Pa.

1936 brought about change on the state level as the Democrats and liberal Republicans seized control of the legislature. With Earle's prodding, they passed the most extensive political reforms in Pennsylvania history. A Department of Public Assistance came into being, private industrial police forces were abolished, a minimum wage law passed, and the state granted labor the right to organize and established a state Labor Relations Board to settle disputes. During the late 1930s, the Steel Workers Organizing Committee and Congress of Industrial Organizations (CIO) formed in

✧

Above: The home of Gifford Pinchot, Milford, Pennsylvania.
COURTESY OF THE AUTHOR.

Below: Not only did industrial workers go on strike during the Depression as pictured here, farm workers near Morrisville in 1938 in the Delaware Valley also protested low wages, harsh conditions, and long hours. Farm owners attempted to break the strike by bringing in black workers to take their jobs.
COURTESY OF THE LIBRARY OF CONGRESS.

Coal Mines

Pennsylvania, unionizing some three hundred thousand men with the support of the state and national governments.

Although twenty percent of Pennsylvanians remained unemployed as late as 1939, thanks to the New Deal, their sufferings were being relieved through public programs. The New Deal brought women, workers, African-Americans, non-Protestants, and the sons and daughters of those who had immigrated from Eastern Europe into the state's political life. For the first time since the Civil War, the Democratic Party became a major factor as it became the dominant party in Pittsburgh, gained ground rapidly in Philadelphia, and established a major presence in the state's smaller cities and industrial regions.

PENNSYLVANIA AT WAR

As the nation's leading industrial and second-most populous state for the first half of the twentieth century, Pennsylvania was indispensable to the victories of the United States in World Wars I and II. Over 370,000 Pennsylvanians served in the First World War, most famously in the renowned 28th Division. Appearing on the Western Front in June, 1918, within four months it fought almost constantly, including at the Battle of Chateau-Thierry and the Second Battle of the Marne: 12,000 of its 25,000 men were wounded and 2,000 killed. On the home front, Charles Schwab of Bethlehem Steel headed the Emergency Fleet Corporation that built most of the vastly expanded United States navy from scratch. His men constructed the world's largest shipyard at Hog Island near Philadelphia; its seven thousand-foot piers could hold twenty-eight vessels at once and extended for two and a half miles. Although it produced the first prefabricated ship in the world, the Hog Island facility was not finished until the war ended.

Thanks to munitions sent to the Allies between 1914 and 1917, when the United States entered the war, Pittsburgh's steel industry had been practically functioning on wartime basis for several years. The Westinghouse Electrical Company was especially active in providing munitions, railroad cars, and other equipment for the Allies. Over 250 factories employed half a million people in war production, many of which operated around the clock. Pittsburgh mills provided four-fifths of the

army's steel, and Pennsylvania mined three-quarters of the coal they used. Philadelphia's Naval Yard and Baldwin Locomotive Works were also among the nation's leaders in producing ships and railroad cars.

Pennsylvania's large German population was opposed to entering the war; there was considerable sympathy for the Central Powers. Governor Martin Brumbaugh (1911-1915) led rallies where German songs were sung and speeches were made wishing for German victories. But once the United States entered on the Allied side, Brumbaugh joined Pennsylvanians in supporting the war. Local officials supported Philadelphia mobs that attacked Socialist meetings—the Socialists were the only significant political group to oppose the war—and arrested the Socialists who defended themselves. With its numerous peace groups, such as Quakers and German groups like the Mennonites, Pennsylvania conscientious objectors were the special targets of popular wrath. Thanks to the war, the Quakers created the American Friends Service Committee to deflect this hostility by providing frequently dangerous and meaningful roles for pacifists as medical workers on the front or at home. In 1947, the group won the Nobel Peace Prize after continuing to work after both world wars to relieve suffering in the war zones.

Pennsylvania was equally essential in World War II. Over a million and a quarter Pennsylvanians, 33,000 of whom died, served in the war; it also had more Medal of Honor winners (32) than any other state. Pennsylvania war leaders included General George C. Marshall, of Uniontown, the army's chief of staff who designed the plan that brought victory to the Allies. He later served as President Truman's Secretary of State from 1947 to 1949 and developed the "Marshall Plan," which offered economic peacetime aid to western European nations with the successful outcome that these prosperous nations did not turn to Communism. Philadelphia admirals Thomas Kincaid and Alan Kirk respectively commanded the Seventh Fleet in the Pacific and the amphibious landing at Normandy Beach. The Landing Ship Tanks used to land troops were developed by the Dravo Corporation Shipyard just north of Pittsburgh: Dravo employed 16,000 workers and manufactured 145 or ten percent of the navy's LSTs.

Over three and a half million Pennsylvanians, nearly half of them women, were employed during a war which brought the economic depression to an end. The Philadelphia Navy Yard alone employed 70,000 people and built over 1,200 ships. That city's Frankford Arsenal manufactured small arms; ordnance works near Williamsport and Meadville produced dynamite. Philadelphia's Quartermaster

✧

Above: "Four Minute Men" spoke in movie theatres and otherwise gave brief lectures urging people to support the war effort during World War I.

COURTESY OF THE LIBRARY OF CONGRESS.

Below and following page: The Works Projects Administration continued to employ artists to produce posters during World War II, but now they sought to involve the public in wartime industries and homeland defense. Volunteers were needed as air raid wardens, auxiliary firemen, and policemen. Another poster advertises that citizens have numerous opportunities to aid the war effort, including collecting scrap metals and growing food in victory gardens.

COURTESY OF THE LIBRARY OF CONGRESS.

Depot was nationally in charge of procuring uniforms for the military. Westinghouse invented the electrically powered torpedo which did not leave a wake for the enemy to trace; the Bantam Car Company of Butler invented the jeep. Pennsylvania industry increased from $5 billion in 1939 to $15 billion in 1944.

However, Pennsylvania industry no longer dominated the nation as it had in World War I and the Civil War. Pittsburgh steel had fallen to thirty-one percent of the nation's total; the state ranked seventh in overall war contracts, fourth in shipbuilding, and third in ordnance. The nation's industrial center of gravity was shifting westward and southward: while Pennsylvania retained its manufacturing importance for another quarter-century, the handwriting was on the wall.

One of the most famous escapes by a slave in United States history occurred in 1849 when Henry Brown shipped himself from Richmond, Virginia, to Philadelphia in a box 3 feet long, 2 1/2 feet deep, and 2 feet wide. Members of the Philadelphia Anti-Slavery Society, including African-American Frederick Douglass, are seen opening the box in this 1850 print.

COURTESY OF THE LIBRARY OF CONGRESS.

THE RESURRECTION OF HENRY BOX BROWN AT PHILADELPHIA.
Who escaped from Richmond Va. in a Box. 3 feet long 2½ ft. deep and 2 ft wide

AFRICAN AMERICANS

The first African Americans came to Philadelphia as slaves in 1684. Most stayed in Philadelphia, where they worked as servants or in trades such as shipbuilding and carpentry. In the country, slave labor was important in the many iron and charcoal furnaces throughout the colony. By the time of the American Revolution, however, Pennsylvania Quakers had started the only anti-slavery movement in what was to become the United States. John Woolman and Anthony Benezet were the most prominent spokesmen against bondage, although the most spectacular was a dwarf named Benjamin Lay, who would disrupt Quaker meetings by pouring out animal blood on the participants to show how the slaves' blood was not only on the hands of slave holders, but on those of everyone who used the products of any laborer who was not a free man. During the Revolution, the Quaker meeting disowned all members who owned slaves, and in 1780, Pennsylvania became the first state to pass a law gradually abolishing slavery. Any slave born after that date would become free when he or she became twenty-eight years old, although people who were already in bondage remained there. Although a handful of blacks remained in slavery as late as 1840, by 1800 almost all had been freed.

Philadelphia also developed the nation's first strong African-American community in the years after the Revolution. Bishop William White not only organized the Episcopal Church, but in 1794, he made an important contribution to black Christianity by ordaining Absalom Jones as the first black deacon, and later priest, in the United States. Jones' church, St. Thomas', opened shortly before Mother Bethel of the African Methodist Episcopal Church, founded by Jones' friend Richard Allen. Guided by former slaves like Allen and Jones, whose masters freed them and whose powerful preaching made them community leaders, the city's blacks flocked to these congregations, where they governed themselves and were not segregated or excluded as in most of the white churches.

Anti-slavery was strong in Pennsylvania. Not only were there strong free black communities along the Maryland border, but the Pennsylvania Abolition Society became famous throughout the nation for defending the rights of blacks whose masters failed to free them as required by law, or who were seized by slaveholders in free states. Legal action was not always sufficient: in 1851 in the town of Christiana, near the Maryland border, slaveholders who attempted to reclaim their "property" were killed in a riot, and those blacks who defended themselves were acquitted on grounds of self-defense. Pennsylvania was also the first state to open a black college, Cheney, in 1854.

Yet as with women who demanded political rights, supporters of African Americans

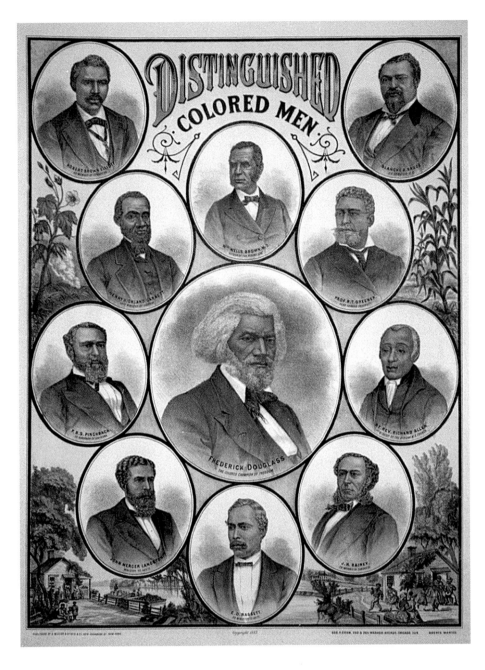

were in the minority. Pennsylvania Hall, a large structure completed in Philadelphia in 1838 to hold abolitionist meetings, was destroyed by a mob only four days after it opened. The rioters were not punished. That year, free blacks who had been allowed to vote by Pennsylvania's Constitution of 1790 lost that right when the state adopted a new Constitution. As with prisoners, the insane, and women, some African Americans in Pennsylvania had benefited from the reforms of the new republic, but they continued to be treated as second-class citizens in both law and popular prejudice.

During the Civil War, Pennsylvania's African Americans fought hard for their freedom. The

✧

Notable American Colored Men. *Published in 1883, this engraving of eleven distinguished black men included only one from the past: Reverend Richard Allen (immediately to the right of Frederick Douglass in the center), who founded the African Methodist Episcopal Church in 1795 and served as its first minister. He is buried in the basement of the current building of the church, "Mother Bethel," at Sixth and Lombard Streets in Philadelphia, which also has a historical exhibit about the church.*
COURTESY OF THE LIBRARY OF CONGRESS.

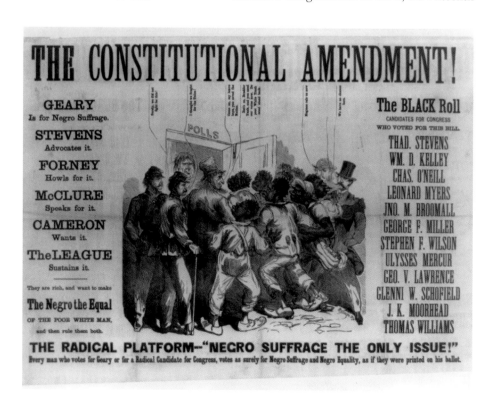

first black soldiers were trained at Camp William Penn near the site of abolitionist Lucretia Mott's home in Elkins Park, just north of Philadelphia. Martin Delany, the first African-American major in the United States army, later moved to South Carolina, where he became a Congressman. In 1870, the Fifteenth Amendment restored the right to vote for Pennsylvania's African Americans, but that achievement was marred when Octavius Catto, a leading black Philadelphia, was murdered for trying to organize voters in 1871. The most notorious lynching in the North, too, occurred in Coatesville, Pennsylvania in 1913.

Pennsylvania's African-American population soared during the years between 1910 and 1920. Philadelphia's rose from 84,000 to over 200,000, and Pittsburgh's from 34,000 to over 50,000. By 1990, over 1,100,000 people, nearly 10 percent of the state's population, were African-American. Many of the newcomers came north to work in the war industries during World War I, a trend repeated in even greater numbers during World War II. Notable African Americans included the first black speaker of a state house of representatives, K. Leroy Irvis, and the first state supreme court chief justice since Reconstruction in the South, Robert N. C. Nix, and Marian Anderson, the first African-American to sing at the Metropolitan Opera House in 1955. Her concert at the Lincoln Memorial in 1939 was the first of many gatherings at that site which marked a landmark in the Civil Rights movement.

SPORTS

No state in the United States has a sports heritage that surpasses Pennsylvania. Baseball's first world series between the National and American Leagues was played in 1903 between the Pittsburgh Pirates and Boston Pilgrims (later the Red Sox). Games four through seven occurred at Exposition Park in Pittsburgh, where the Pirates played until moving to Forbes Field, the first ballpark made completely of concrete and steel, in 1919. Boston won the best five out of nine games. The greatest Pirate ballplayer of these early days was shortstop Honus Wagner, who lived his entire life in Carnegie, Pennsylvania. He played for the team from 1900 to 1917, winning the National League batting championship eight times, and coached for the Pirates from 1933 to 1951. He was one of the first five players elected to the Baseball Hall of Fame in 1936.

Another Pennsylvanian, Christy Mathewson, was also among these five. Born in 1880 in Factoryville in Wyoming County, Mathewson attended Bucknell Univesity in Lewisburg, where he was also an outstanding football player and president of his class. After graduating, he joined the New York Giants, where he won 373 games and lost only 138; his greatest moment came in the 1905 World Series, when he shut out the Philadelphia Athletics three times in six days and only allowed fourteen hits. A moral paragon who did not drink, smoke, or pitch on Sundays, Mathewson enlisted in World War I, where he inhaled poisoned gas; he came down with tuberculosis and died in 1925.

The Pittsburgh team began as the Alleghenies in 1887, and were renamed the Pirates in 1891 after they "stole" Louis Bierbauer from the Philadelphia Athletics. In 1901 they won their first league championship, and the following year repeated with a record of 103 wins and 36 losses. Among their other accomplishments, the Pirates were the first team to put a tarpaulin on the infield when it rained in 1906. Other great Pirates included Ralph Kiner, later the long-time broadcaster for the New York Mets, who won the national league home run title every year from 1946 to 1952, Willie Stargell (who hit a club record 475 home runs), Robert Clemente, only the eleventh player in major league history to make 3,000 hits, four-time national league batting champion in his eighteen year career, who tragically died in a plane crash while delivering emergency aid to earthquake victims in Nicaragua in 1972. The Pirates also won one of the most dramatic World Series in modern times in 1960, with Bill Mazeroski hitting a game-winning home run in the ninth inning of the seventh game to defeat the New York Yankees.

✧

Jim Thorpe, voted the greatest athlete in the United States for the first half of the twentieth century, in one of his many guises: as a baseball player for the New York Giants. He attended the Indian School in Carlisle, Pennsylvania and is now buried in the town named for him, formerly Mauch Chunk.
COURTESY OF THE LIBRARY OF CONGRESS.

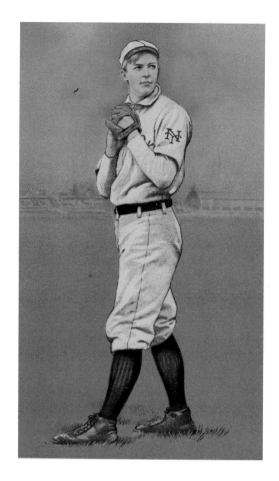

Top, left: Honus Wagner (1874-1955). Native of Pittsburgh and shortstop for the Pittsburgh Pirates, was one of the greatest baseball players of all time. Along with Pennsylvania native and New York Giants pitcher Christy Mathewson (1880-1925) he was one of the first five men inducted into the Baseball Hall of Fame.

Top, right: Mathewson, a graduate of Bucknell University in Lewisburg, refused to pitch on Sundays, drink, or swear. He enlisted in the army in World War I and died from tuberculosis contracted after gas poisoning at an early age.

COURTESY OF THE LIBRARY OF CONGRESS.

Below: Manager of the Philadelphia Athletics from 1901 to 1950, Connie Mack (1862-1953) as depicted on his 1910 baseball card, originally played catcher and became part-owner of the team. He managed two of the greatest teams in baseball history, the "$100,000 infield" (referring to their combined salaries) in the first decade of the twentieth century and three-time league champions from 1928-1930. His record for the most wins by any major league manager and the duration of his tenure will probably never be challenged.

COURTESY OF THE LIBRARY OF CONGRESS.

The Pittsburgh area's African-American teams were perhaps even better than the Pirates. Founded in 1912, the Homestead Grays entered the Negro National League in 1936; from 1937 to 1945 they won the League championship nine years in a row. They played many of their home games in Forbes Field, and others in Griffith Stadium, home of the Washington Senators in the District of Columbia. Their star, known as the "Black Babe Ruth," was Josh Gibson (1911-1947), who hit over 800 home runs in the Negro leagues in a career he spent with the Homestead Grays and Pittsburgh Crawfords from 1930 to 1946. Elected to the Hall of Fame in 1972, he was the only man ever to hit a fair ball out of Yankee Stadium. Other stars of the Crawfords included pitchers "Cool Papa" Bell and "Satchel Paige," who finally played a few games in the integrated major leagues very late in his career. Philadelphia's black team, the Stars, never won a championship.

Philadelphia's baseball teams, the Athletics (who moved to Kansas City in 1955) and the Phillies have also made sports history. Connie Mack managed the Athletics, of which he was part owner, from 1901 until 1950, a record that is likely to stand forever. His teams that won the America League pennant from 1929 to 1931 are considered among the greatest of all time. The Athletics moved to Kansas City in 1955. The Phillies, on the other hand, are best remembered for their many years of hard luck. It took them 33 years, from their founding in 1883 until 1915, to reach the World Series. But between 1917 and 1949 they only finished as high as fourth in the eight-team National League once, in 1932. During World War II, they finished last every season except one (when they finished seventh), barely managed 1000 fans per game, and had to be subsidized by the other National League clubs because no one would buy them. They won the National League pennant in 1950 and three Eastern Division titles in the 1970s before winning the World Series in 1980, after 97 years of play, and won another division championship in 1993. Among their greatest players since the 1950s were pitchers Robin Roberts and Steve Carlton, who won four Cy Yong Awards, outfielders Richie Allen and Richie Ashburn, and infielder Pete Rose. Mike Schmidt won the national league home run title seven times.

Pennsylvania is also the home to Little League Baseball. Carl Stoltz developed the idea in Williamsport in 1938; the first twelve Little League World Series were held there from 1947 to 1958. Truly a World Series today, thousands of teams from many nations now compete as opposed to the three teams that played twenty-four games during the first season. When asked about his prowess in baseball at Yale University, President George W. Bush responded "I peaked in Little League."

Pennsylvania has always been a basketball power as well. In the twenties, teams such as the Pottsville Maroons were among the best in the nation, along with the Williamsport Millionaires.

In footbal, the Philadelphia Eagles were originally the Frankford Yellowjackets and took their present name in 1933 to honor the "Eagle" that symbolized the New Deal's National Recovery Administration. Their general manager Bert Bell came up with the idea of the college draft in 1935 to equalize talent, and had the honor of drafting the first player in 1936. In 1939 the Eagles played the Brooklyn Dodgers (also a football team at the time) in the first televised game in football history. During 1943, with most eligible players in the military, the Eagles and Pittsburgh Steelers merged briefly to become the Steagles. The Eagles won their first National League championship in 1948, second in 1970, and third in 2005 although they have yet to win the Superbowl. Quarterback Ron Jaworski and defensive end Reggie White were probably the Eagles' greatest players. The Steelers, on the other hand, after

wining only 22 games in their first seven seasons, went on to win four Superbowls in the 1970s starring the famous Front Four defensive line including Franco Harris and "Mean" Joe Greene, led by quarterback Ron Jaworski. Pittsburgh also signed the first "big money" player in the history of the game, Byron "Whizzer" White in 1936, who later became a justice of the United States Supreme Court. Also worth mentioning is Joe Paterno, Penn State University's head football coach since 1966, who, as of 2007, had won 373 games, the most of any Division One coach in college history. Paterno's support of academics (especially the Department of Classics and the Library named after him and his wife Sue) is unprecedented by any college sports coach.

Pennsylvania is also famous as the site of the annual Head of the Schuylkill rowing classic in Philadelphia; a statue commemorates 1920 and 1924 Olympic Champion Jack Kelly, father of Princess Grace of Monaco. No other set of boat-

❖

Above: Statue of Joe Paterno on the Penn State University Campus. At the age of 81, he has been head coach since 1966. He has especially distinguished himself for his interest in the academic progress of his students and his philanthropy to the university, which has named its new library after him and his wife.

COURTESY OF THE AUTHOR.

Left: Glenn "Pop" Warner, who made the Carlisle Indian School and coached Jim Thorpe into a national football power.

COURTESY OF THE LIBRARY OF CONGRESS.

houses in the world are as beautiful as those north of the Art Museum: in 1858, eight boathouses formed the "Schuylkill Navy" to promote amateur rowing, the first such body in America. They still sit on Kelly Drive.

The Penn Relays, held annually since 1896 at the University of Pennsylvania, is the nation's leading collegiate track meet, with over twenty-thousand competitors now participating over three days. Pennsylvania's contribution to the sport of golf is Arnold Palmer, voted the Associated Press' Athlete of the Decade for the 1960s and winner of 92 tournaments. Born in 1929, Palmer played his final professional tournament in 2005.

A list of leading professional sports figures associated with Pennsylvania goes on and on: Wilt Chamberlain of the Philadelphia 76s, the only person to score 100 points in a professional basketball game and the sport's all-time leading scorer with over 31,000 points; quarterbacks Johnny Unitas of the Baltimore Colts and Joe Namath of the New York Jets, who squared off against each other in Superbowl III; Pete Gray, a one-armed outfielder who played briefly for the Chicago White Sox during the manpower shortage of World War II; catcher Roy Campanella of the Brooklyn Dodgers, who was tragically crippled in an automobile accident; Stan Musial, outfielder for the St. Louis Cardinals, from Donora; early tennis star Bill Tilden; pool shooter Willie Mosconi; oddsmaker Jimmy the Greek; and last but not least, Smarty Jones, the racehorse from Philadelphia Park who won the Preakness and Kentucky Derby before losing the Belmont Stakes in 2004.

But perhaps the greatest of all athletes associated with Pennsylvania is Jim Thorpe (1888-1953). This part Sac and Fox Indian, who was born in Indian territory the year before it became the state of Oklahoma, was recognized as the greatest football player and American athlete of the first half of the twentieth century by the Associated Press. His beginnings were humble. In 1903, his father sent him to the Carlisle Indian School in Pennsylvania, where he met the legendary "Pop" Warner, the school's athletic director from 1899 to 1904 and again from 1907 to 1914. Under Warner's tutelage, Thorpe won the decathlon and pentathlon at the 1912 Olympic Games in Stockholm; he became a national hero and was welcomed home to the United States with a tickertape parade in New York City. At the same time, he was the halfback and star of Carlisle's football team, which regularly beat Ivy League Schools as Warner developed many of the plays used in football until this day. Warner later coached nine years (1915-1924) at the University of Pittsburgh before moving to California.

Thorpe's last years were tragic. Stripped of his Olympic medals because he had made a few dollars playing amateur baseball, he played professional baseball and football for several teams between 1913 and 1928 before working as a movie extra and construction worker in Los Angeles. Upon his death, his wife arranged for him to be buried in Mauch Chunk, Pennsylvania, a town that changed its name to Jim Thorpe in his honor.

Sociologists attribute the great interest in sports in Pennsylvania to the large number of youngsters who grew up in the coal and steel towns and inner cities, for whom professional football, baseball, and basketball seemed the best way to escape their grim communities. It remains to be seen whether Pennsylvanians will continue to shine disproportionately in sports in the post-industrial age.

The Wissahickon, whose beauty inspired
Edgar Allen Poe.
COURTESY OF THE AUTHOR.

LITERATURE

Pennsylvania's first great writer was none other than William Penn himself. Writing pamphlets defending Quakers' right to worship and persuading people to emigrate to America, Penn published dozens of works. His most meaningful for us today is his book of maxims, *Fruits of Solitude*, which contains thoughts for people to live peaceably together, and a plan that foreshadowed the idea of a United Nations where nations would come together and do likewise. During the colonial era, Benjamin Franklin did more than invent the Franklin stove, bifocals, and harness electricity, he was British North America's foremost writer. His autobiography is the classic story of the poor boy who makes good through hard work and natural ability; *Poor Richard's Almanac* dispensed folk wisdom and glorified the average person who read it at the expense of kings, aristocrats, lawyers, and other upper-class types. Less known than Franklin is William Moraley, who lived both in Pennsylvania and New Jersey. His life-story, *The Infortunate*, is the entertaining tale of a man who not only had bad luck but was led astray by companions and strong drink to squander those opportunities he had—Benjamin Franklin in reverse.

Early on Pennsylvania was the new nation's literary capital. Along with Franklin, Pennsylvania had come to symbolize the new nation. Michel Guillaume de Crèvecoeur pretended to be a farmer from Carlisle when he wrote *Letters from an American Farmer*, published in 1782. He demonstrated how "the American…a new man" (or woman, for he named his daughter "America") could rise from "idleness, servile dependence, penury, and useless labor" in Europe to "ample subsistence" on the Pennsylvania frontier. Charles Brockden Brown was the first American who tried to earn his living, unsuccessfully, as a novelist. Perhaps his most powerful work, *Arthur Mervyn*, reinforced the national myth of the city as a den of temptation for humble farm boys who go there—in this case Philadelphia—and encounter numerous disreputable but colorful characters. Hugh Henry Brackenridge, a western Pennsylvania legislator and judge, wrote the satirical *American Chivalry* in which a Captain Farrago (modeled on Don Quixote), a would-be frontier aristocrat, persuades his henchman Teague O'Regan (modeled on Sancho Panza) to follow his political lead. All these works are still in print after more than two centuries.

So is *The Quaker City*, or *The Monks of Monks Hall*, written in 1847 by Pennsylvanian George Lippard. One of the most popular American novels of the early nineteenth century, this gothic tale recounts the moral depths to which William Penn's "Holy Experiment" had supposedly fallen. Virtuous women Mary and Becky are seduced by the evil Lorrimer as the "monks" reduce true religion to a mockery. Later in the century, Philadelphian Owen Wister wrote *The Virginian*, but never finished *Romney*, a novel that might have depicted the snobbery and romantic secrets of late-nineteenth century Philadelphia high society much as Edith Wharton did for New York City. A short story by Edgar Allan Poe, *Morning on the Wissahickon*, survives from his unsuccessful effort to start a literary magazine in Philadelphia: he reminds us that if this creek were located seven miles from London instead, this beautiful stream would be immortalized in literature like Shakespeare's River Avon.

Perhaps the greatest philosopher in American history, Charles Sanders Peirce, lived the last 27 years of his life in a rambling old mansion he named Arisbe on the outskirts of Milford, Pennsylvania. The founder of pragmatism, Peirce devoted his life to questioning the beliefs his contemporaries considered certain. People could never know anything for certain, he insisted, but only from a particular perspective, what "worked" for them. This idea, called "pragmatism," was adopted by William James and John Dewey

and is considered the most important American contribution to philosophy. Peirce also questioned Darwinism as applied to society: he did not think modern America was the best of all societies that had evolved naturally out of history, but that change, when it did occur, was catastrophic and not necessarily for the best.

In modern times, the best Pennsylvania writers have given us vivid portrayals of the lives of ordinary people. John O'Hara's *Samaria* is really Pottsville. *Ten North Frederick*, the title of one novel, is in fact the house he grew up in down the block from the Yuengling Brewery on Mahantongo Street. John Updike's *Rabbit* books tell the story of a boyhood in Shillington, a middle-class suburb of Reading. Annie Dillard's *An American Girlhood* warmly evokes Pittsburgh in the 1940s and 50s. Thomas Bell's *Out of This Furnace* offers the story of several generations of a family that began as Slavic immigrants and struggled to survive in the steel mills around Pittsburgh. Conrad Richter's *Light in the Forest* is the tale of a white boy, kidnapped by Indians at the time of the French and Indian War, who grows to love the society that captured him.

Pennsylvania is also known for historical writing. David McCullough, perhaps the best-known popular historian of our time, began his career by writing about the Johnstown Flood, which occurred near his birthplace in western Pennsylvania. John Lukacs, a Hungarian immigrant who has lived near Philadelphia since the end of World War II, is not only one of the leading historians of that war, but has written both critically and lovingly of Philadelphia in a book of that title and his autobiographical *Confessions of an Original Sinner*. And in the 1970s, Professors Stephanie Grauman Wolfe of the University of Delaware and Richard Dunn of the University of Pennsylvania established the Philadelphia (now McNeil—named for donor Robert L. McNeil, Jr.) Center for Early American Studies. The McNeil Center, along with the Omohundro Institute at Colonial Williamsburg, Virginia, lead the nation's scholarly community in exploring our colonial and revolutionary past.

ART

The history of American art would be much poorer without Pennsylvania's contribution. The most vivid surviving pictures of American Indians that date from the colonial period were painted by Gustav Hesselius at the request of Proprietor John Penn, and may be found at the Historical Society of Pennsylvania. Moravian Johan Haidt executed the spectacular *The First Fruits*, which hangs in the Moravian Archives at Bethlehem. It depicts people all over the world, including Africans, and American Indians, converted by this most zealous group of Christian missionaries. And while Quakers shunned portrait painting as vanity—aside from a youthful portrait before he converted, only one pencil sketch of William Penn taken without his knowledge survives—numerous portraits of Benjamin Franklin show his many sides; he preferred to be painted in a fur cap in France to demonstrate the natural, down-to-earth American, but while in Pennsylvania and England he made sure he wore a wig and elegant clothes to show that he was a workingman no more, but rather a successful gentleman.

When the American Revolution ended in triumph, Philadelphia's Charles Willson Peale made sure that the heroes who made this possible were remembered by posterity. He began the nation's first museum in 1786. It contained not only animal specimens peculiar to the New World, including bones of a giant mastodon, but also portraits of George Washington, Thomas Jefferson, and numerous other famous men. Timothy Matlack, a leader of the Philadelphia workingmen, who wore a worker's cap, stands out from all the rest. Peale was also instrumental in beginning America's longest-lived school of art, the Pennsylvania Academy of Fine Arts, now located at Broad and Cherry Streets in a building opened in 1876.

As the 1800s progressed, pictures of everyday life supplanted the portraits commissioned by the wealthy as the best works of art available. John Lewis Krimmel's lively crowd scenes are among the most vivid recreations of early nineteenth century life that survive. As factories and railroads became more frequent, Americans turned to landscape paintings that showed the American "garden" could comfortably accommodate the "machine." The Pennslyvania landscapes of George Hetzel are outstanding in this respect.

In the years after the Civil War, Pennsylvania's Thomas Hovenden and Frederick Rothermel became famous for their vast historical canvases. The world imagines the Battle of Gettysburg primarily through

Rothermel's monumental depiction of the battle that sits on the floor of the Pennsylvania State Museum (it was too large to hang on the wall), although it is a composite of several scenes from that epic three-day struggle rather than a literal depiction of any one moment. Pennsylvania's greatest painters of the age, however, were Thomas Eakins and Mary Cassatt. Eakins' realism appears at its best in *The Gross Clinic*, where an anatomy professor dissects a corpse before an audience of students. It hangs at the Thomas Jefferson Hospital in Philadelphia. Allowing female students to sketch male nudes from life, however, caused him to lose his position at the Pennsylvania Academy. The sister of the President of the Pennsylvania Railroad, Cassatt is the only American, and only woman painter, ever recognized as an equal by the leading group of male painters in the world. The French Impressionists had such regard for Cassatt and her paintings of young women and children (she never married herself and had no children) that they became ranked with Monet's water lilies and Degas' ballet dancers as among the most easily recognizable paintings in history.

Cassatt lived most of her life in France, as did Philadelphia's Henry Osswa Tanner, the leading black painter in America before 1900. After executing some excellent examples of African-American life for which there was no market, Tanner also moved to Paris, where he devoted most of his life to religious works that made him a wealthy man. Other important black artists are Meta Fuller, a sculptress whose busts of black women are both beautiful and powerful, and Horace Pippin, a self-educated folk artist from West Chester. Pippin is remembered mostly for his warm and evocative scenes of local life, although his most powerful works indict "Mr. Prejudice" and show scenes of World War I, in which he was wounded.

Pennsylvania's twentieth-century art has especially embodied its industrial heritage. Excellent industrial art can be found in two major collections: the Westmoreland County Museum of Art in Greensburg, where scenes of industrial life in a particular place are juxtaposed with earlier landscape paintings of the same spot, and the Steidle Museum of Art at the Pennsylvania State University, where many paintings show the beauty, as well as the devastation of industrial landscapes. Two notable museums in Pittsburgh are the Andy Warhol, which honors that city's "pop artist," whose repetitious works (most famously the can of Campbell's soup) made fun of the monotony of modern life; and the nearby Mattress Factory, which houses changing exhibitions of experimental art that integrates sculpture, painting, and performance through electronic media. Mural projects in Pittsburgh, Philadelphia (which has several hundred), State College, York, and other cities show how contemporary Pennsylvania remains a vital presence in the world of artistic creation.

Mill St. June 2d

DISASTERS

Pennsylvania's leading role in the industrialization of America came at a great price. For much of their history, the state's coal mines were not only dangerous, but at times, death traps. Three of the great mine disasters took place in Luzerne County. The first was at Avondale, near Wilkes Barre, which occurred in 1869. A fire broke out, killing 110 people, including five boys between the ages of twelve and seventeen. The coal company had built a breaker where coal was sorted directly on top of the mine, which led to its collapse. Amazingly, although the disaster caused the Pennsylvania legislature to forbid building breakers directly over mines, Luzerne County's state representative ensured that his own county, whose very tragedy had inspired the law, was exempted from it on the grounds it would hamper the economy. The Twin Shaft Disaster of 1896 at Pittston killed 58 men in a cave-in. They had no chance of escaping, as the mine only had one narrow escape shaft. The lack of concern for its employees' safety of the Newton Coal Company, that owned the mine, provided a powerful stimulus to the United Mine Workers' successful effort to unionize the region a few years later. As late as 1959, however, safety regulations were being ignored: the Knox Coal Company, controlled by organized crime, not only used non-union labor but ignored state laws that forbade tunneling coal mines under rivers. At Port Griffith, pressure from the Susquehanna River caused a mine to collapse, killing twelve men when over ten billion gallons of water flooded in.

Not all of the state's disasters occurred in Luzerne County. The Hartwick Mine Explosion of 1904 in a bituminous mine near Pittsburgh claimed 181 lives. As a result, Andrew Carnegie founded the Carnegie Hero Fund Commission to reward rescuers who placed their own lives at risk— or to compensate their families if they died. The Marianna disaster four years later inflicted 154 deaths on a mining community praised for its welfare measures. And since 1962, at Centralia in Columbia County, a fire spewing smoke and sulfur dioxide has been smoldering in an old coal pit that was converted into a landfill. Some residents still refuse to leave; the fire may well burn for another hundred years. Centralia's ruins symbolize the decline of Pennsylvania's mining industry and the environmental devastation that marks much of the state's coal region.

Just as noteworthy as the state's mining disasters is the Johnstown Flood of 1889, whose victims are today honored by a museum in that city. Eight inches of rain fell during May 30-31 of that year, causing the South Fork Dam, constructed in the 1840s to hold back Lake Conemaugh, to burst. Andrew Carnegie and his partners were among the members of the South Fork Fishing and Hunting Club which had purchased the lake in 1879 and failed to make repairs to the dam despite repeated warnings. Flowing at fifty miles per hour, a thirty-six foot high wall of water rushed into Johnstown, killing 2,200 people and destroying most of the town. Between 1938 and 1943, in response to another flood in 1936, the United States Army Corps of Engineers built a nine-mile

✧

Aftermath of the Johnstown Flood of 1889.

Top: The famous Johnstown Flood of 1889. Someone with a dark sense of humor labeled the photograph "a slightly damaged house."
COURTESY OF THE LIBRARY OF CONGRESS.

Middle: In 1908, the Marianna Coal Mine in Westmoreland County exploded because of underground gas, killing 154 people. Opened in 1907, it was a considered a model "patch" town throughout the United States for working conditions and was visited by president Theodore Roosevelt.
COURTESY OF THE GEORGE GRAHAM BAIN COLLECTION, LIBRARY OF CONGRESS.

Bottom: The first railroad bridge across the Susquehanna at Harrisburg burned in 1844. Mrs. T. Schreiner executed this lithograph in 1845.
COURTESY OF THE O'CONNOR/YAEGER COLLECTION, PALMER MUSEUM, PENN STATE UNIVERSITY. IN CLEAR FOLDER.

channel alongside the three rivers that flow together near Johnstown, effectively eliminating serious danger from floods.

Pennsylvania's leadership in the nation's nuclear power industry—the first operating plant in the United States opened in Shippingsport in 1957—contributed to the near-disaster of Three Mile Island, just south of Harrisburg on the Susquehanna River. On March 28, 1979, workers accidentally shut off the supply of water that cooled one of two reactors. Although the reactor shut down, pressure built up from the water and a relief valve stuck open and allowed radioactive coolant water to escape. About one-third of the nuclear core melted down. Before the problem was fixed, 200,000 Pennsylvanians fled their homes, and the plant came within an hour of releasing the equivalent of several hydrogen bombs. Although no fatalities or even diseases or injuries can be traced to the incident, Three Mile Island became a symbol throughout the world for the hazards of nuclear power: people all over the globe began to wear t-Shirts stating "We All Live in Pennsylvania."

Six years later, a man-made disaster of a different sort struck Philadelphia. For the second time in American history (the first was Tulsa, Oklahoma during a race riot in 1917), an African-American

The Johnstown Calamity
A slightly damaged house.

community was bombed by order of the city's own officials, in this case black mayor Wilson Goode. The radical group MOVE, living at 6221 Osage Avenue in West Philadelphia, had frequent confrontations with the police and disturbed other residents of their predominantly middle-class African-American neighborhood with their noisy and unhygienic style of living. When negotiations with the city broke down, a helicopter dropped a bomb on the house. When the fire it started was extinguished, eleven people including five children were dead, fifty-three houses destroyed, and 262 people left homeless.

More recently, Pennsylvania has been the site of the tragic yet inspiring crash of Flight 93. When Taliban terrorists hijacked that plane out of Boston's Logan Airport on September 11, 2001, the passengers, learning through cellphone communications of the destruction of the Twin Towers, seized the plane from their captors and forced it to land, killing all aboard, near Shanksville, Pennsylvania, in Somerset County. An arbor of trees now commemorates the event, the latest of the disasters in which Pennsylvania has shown the ability of public-spirited citizens to survive and triumph over the natural and man-made catastrophes which have been an important part of its history.

Pennsylvania Today:
Recovering the Past
and Looking to the Future

As the year 2000 approached, Brent Glass, who was then the executive director of the Pennsylvania Historical and Museum Commission, decided to mark the coming millennium with a new history of the state. Thanks to the historical-mindedness of thousands of Pennsylvanians, who paid an extra $20 for automobile license plates bearing images of the Pennsylvania Railroad or the Battleship *Niagara*, the Commission was able to hire seventeen prominent scholars and publish a book of 650 pages with 500 illustrations that sold for the modest sum of $50 in hardback, $30 in paper. No censorship of any kind was imposed; instead the commission provided all the assistance it could and urged the scholars to do their best.

✧

*Tina Williams Brewer's 1996 Story Quilt:
Yo Blood Line, draws richly on African-
American symbolism to illustrate themes of
American history. This Pittsburgh native,
like many other Pennsylvanians, keeps alive
the state's quilting tradition.*

COURTESY OF THE STATE MUSEUM OF PENNSYLVANIA,
PENNSYLVANIA HISTORICAL AND MUSEUM COMMISSION

Founded in 1913, the State Historical and Museum Commission (PHMC) is one of the wonders of public history in the United States. It manages the state archives and over fifty museum sites and supports public and private organizations engaged in advancing history—such as the journal *Pennsylvania History*—based on the advice of scholarly boards rather than partisan pressure. Its oral historian, Linda Shopes, has served as president of the nation's oral history association; its curator of photography Linda Ries has won the American Library Association's annual award for the best publication of new archival material in the nation, a special issue of *Pennsylvania History* on Pennsylvania's photographic history. The PHMC not only provides assistance to researchers; it offers them fellowships to use its resources. Its employees do more than help others. They are important scholars whom the state has paid to publish their own work for nearly a century. The state not only marks historical sites; it hires professional historians to devel-

op a website that explains their significance and offers lesson plans that enable teachers from kindergarten through college the opportunity to use them in connection with pictures and documents to teach Pennsylvania history (explorepahistory.com).

What is most striking about Pennsylvania's devotion to its history is the extent to which public and private agencies cooperate and the effort of nearly all concerned to present history that does not pressure people into a pre-determined opinion. For instance, the National Constitution Center in Philadelphia, funded largely through private donations on public land, opened in 2003 as a museum in which different views of constitutional issues are presented and visitors are encouraged to make up their own minds through readings, photographs, artifacts, and interactive exhibits. Religious organizations such as Christ and St. Peter's Episcopal Churches, the Jewish Congregation Mikveh Israel and Museum of Jewish History, the Friends' Meeting House, and the African-American Museum located beside and within Independence Historical National Park present their own programs to further knowledge of their role in the nation's past that seamlessly dovetail with the efforts of the city, state, and national government. Visitors to Johnstown can experience the flood (vicariously, of course; tourists at the Anthracite Museum in Scranton or at Eckley's Miners Village can descend into a mine, or spend an afternoon in a simulated patch town) constructed in the 1980s for the film *The Molly Maguires*.

Heritage tourism has become one of Pennsylvania's leading industries in the twenty-first century. For a state whose population has barely grown in the past twenty years, and in which some areas are largely memorials to industries which no longer flourish—there is a Ghost Town Trail of coal towns in the southwestern part of the state—Pennsylvania's glory and identity rest largely with its history. To be sure, Pennsylvania has its share of new industries—the state abounds in public and private colleges, hospitals and medical schools, and suburban Philadelphia is a bastion of high technology—but much of the state remains a memorial to different phases of its history.

✧

Altoona. 1988. Kevin Kutz (b. 1955) artist. Oil on canvas 60" × 60". A whimsical view of this historical town.

COURTESY OF THE MARGERY WOLFE KUHN ART ACQUISITION ENDOWMENT FUND, COLLECTION OF THE SOUTHERN ALLEGHENIES MUSEUM OF ART.

✧

Left: Jack Savitzky (1910-1992) was a Pennsylvania folk artist. His 1982 rendition of The William Penn Treaty *puts the Indians at the center, makes their height equal to the colonists, and shows the colonists asking them for land in a territory where no houses had been built. Contrast this with the print of the Benjamin West painting.*
STATE MUSEUM OF PENNSYLVANIA, PENNSYLVANIA HISTORICAL AND MUSEUM COMMISSION

Below: Some modern Pennsylvania products: (left to right). Mazza Vineyards (northeast)—Pennsylvania produces many fine wines but does not sell them outside the state; Pfaltzgraff china (York) ; Martin Guitar (Nazareth); Slinky (James Industries, Hollidaysburg); Mr. Rogers Trolley (Holgate Toys, Kane; Mr. Rogers was a Pittsburgh television personality); Berks Bologna (Reading); Boyd's Bears (Gettysburg); Crayola Crayons (Easton); Wos Wit Chow Chow (Grouse Hunt Farms, Tamaqua); Lucky Leaf Applesauce (Knouse Foods, Peach Glen); Heinz 57 Sauce (Pittsburgh); Hershey bar (Hershey); Philadelphia Cream Cheese (Kraft foods, Allentown); Wilbur Buds (Lititz); Mrs. T's Perogies, (Sheandoah); Woolrich Stag Jacket (Woolrich); Utz Potato Chips (Hanover); University Creamery Ice Cream (Penn State University); Iron City Beer (Pittsburgh); Yuengling Beer (Pottsville); Wilton Armetale (Mount Joy). Many of these are food products linked to the state's Pennsylvania German and Slavic heritage. As of 2005, agriculture was Pennsyylania's leading industry; tourism second; and manufacturing third. In 1900, steel ranked first; coal second; oil third.
COURTESY OF THE STATE MUSEUM OF PENNSYLVANIA, HISTORICAL AND MUSEUM COMMISSION.

Bucks and Chester County farmhouses evoke the eighteenth century; parts of downtown Philadelphia minus its cars still resemble the city of Benjamin Franklin; abandoned coal mines and factories recall the state's industrial greatness, as do the still–surviving nineteenth-century mansions and middle-class houses where those who profited from that wealth lived; forests again dominate much of the state's landscape, as hunters and fishermen flock to thin stocks of animals who have lost all their natural predators except for human beings. Most of the past three hundred years of American history survive in Pennsylvania, which will always be remembered for its distinctive contributions to development of religious toleration, political democracy and industrial growth in the modern world.

Lime Kiln (Lime Plant). Ethel Herrick

Warwick, artist. Before 1937.

Chestnut Hill, Philadelphia. 20" × 34".

Oil on canvas.

HISTORIC PENNSYLVANIA

SHARING THE HERITAGE

historic profiles of businesses, organizations,

and families that have contributed

to the development and economic base

of Pennsylvania

BACHMANN INDUSTRIES

Bachmann Industries, known today for its realistic model railroad equipment, began in 1833 as a manufacturer of products made of horn, ivory, and tortoise shell. The firm was founded by Henry Carlisle who specialized in producing fashionable high-back Spanish combs used by women of that era to keep their long hair in place. The combs were especially popular with ladies in the South, although that business deteriorated following the Civil War.

To compensate for loss of the Spanish comb business, Carlisle turned to the manufacture of side combs, dressing combs, barrettes and other hair ornaments made from both horn and tortoise shell. The firm also produced ivory umbrella handles.

Meanwhile, a similar business operated by Henry G. Bachmann and his son, Walter J. Bachmann, was prospering in Philadelphia. Bachmann was a master woodcarver who also worked in tortoise shell, amber, and ivory, and won top prizes in the Centennial Exposition of 1876. At the time, another son, Henry E. Bachman, was managing the business of Henry Carlisle and the two firms agreed to a merger in 1899.

The business was located at 609 Commerce Street in Philadelphia, directly in front of Independence Hall. The site is now an underground parking lot.

In 1902, with a total workforce of sixteen and annual sales of less than $200,000, the company began the manufacture of ladies'

side combs made of a new material called celluloid, which was the first known plastic. However, women began to 'bob' their hair around 1910 and this change in feminine hair fashions soon put an end to the side comb business.

To cope with the shifting fashions, the Bachmanns turned to a new product. In 1912 the company started manufacturing eyeglass frames made of celluloid, which was referred to in the optical trade as 'zylonite.' The firm was the second in the nation to manufacture celluloid or so-called tortoise-shell optical frames.

Henry G. Bachmann died in 1914 and left the business to his two sons, who promptly changed the name to Bachmann Brothers. The company moved to a more spacious Philadelphia facility at 1400 East Erie Avenue in 1929, a location it still occupies today.

Bachmann Brothers was a pioneer in the process of injection molding and construction was started on two floors of the new location in order to satisfy demand

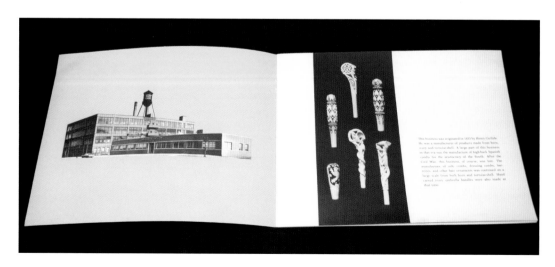

for mass production. The year 1937 was a banner year for the company, thanks to the production of frames in a variety of colors for prescription sunglasses.

With the outbreak of World War II, the Bachmann Brothers turned much of its capacity toward the war effort. The company produced large quantities of protective eye devices, along with submarine battery caps, sunglasses, black powder bags, even desk set holders for ink bottles and fountain pens. Additional floors were added to the Erie Avenue building to meet the urgent need for more space.

In 1943, J.C. Crowther and B.H. Crowther, nephews of the Bachmanns, assumed control of the growing business.

Although Bachmann was a pioneer in the development of injection molding and produced millions of sunglasses, the company's greatest impact on the average person came with a simple product—a toy. Anyone who has ever played with model trains knows the importance of the train village and Bachmann made the villages.

Plasticville U.S.A., which was first produced in 1947, was born as a result of the new process of injection molding. First came rustic fences, then picket fences. They were soon followed with a variety of "assemble it yourself" kits of houses, stores, and other plastic replicas that enhanced train layouts. All were manufactured in the popular 'O' gauge size used by the most popular

✧

Bachmann became a leader in the growing model railroading hobby.

✧

*Above: Bachmann's snap-fit E-Z Track®
revolutionized model railroading*

*Below: Kader Industrial, Ltd., made the first
model trains for Bachmann's American
market, later acquiring Bachmann
Industries in 1981.*

electric trains of the period—the smaller 'HO'
scale came later.

Plasticville featured a 'snap-together'
construction with 'no glue necessary' and these
attributes made them a favorite choice of
parents who gave the kits to their children
along with electric trains for the holiday season.

The line became an overnight success
and created a need for more space so, once again,
another floor was added for shipping and offices.

Bachman Industries' product line expanded
during the 1950s and early 1960s. A product
list from that period included car battery caps
produced for Exide and Ford; Par-T-Ware
brand products including favor baskets, cake
decorations and candleholders; infant feeding
utensils; kitchen utensils, cigar holders, poker
chips, reading glasses and sunglasses.

Toy and hobby lines were expanded to
include high quality 'N' scale electric trains
and battery-operated toys. Meanwhile, the
company continued to produce large numbers
of the popular Plasticville villages.

Bachmann soon became the largest
manufacturer of sunglasses in the world. One
of the lines—Stein Erickson—was reputed to
be the finest skiing glasses produced at that
time. The glasses had interchangeable lenses
that could adapt to varying conditions of
sunlight and reflections and were used by
Olympic Ski teams. In addition, Bachmann
produced Winchester shooting glasses, Doug
Sanders golfing glasses, and even special
sunglasses for fishing. In the safety glass field,
Bachmann's industrial Lexan glasses exceeded
government standards by fifty percent.

The glasses became a hit in Hollywood and
were worn in movies by such stars as Sophia
Loren. They even attracted the attention of the
famous entertainment impresario Walt
Disney, who authorized special edition
sunglasses with a rifle rim piece and
advertised them weekly on his highly popular
Daniel Boone television show. In 1956, Disney
paid a personal visit to the Bachmann
plant on Erie Avenue to see how the glasses
were manufactured.

The plastics industry hit its peak in the
1960s and Bachmann Industries maximized
its opportunities. One shop employee could
operate eight injection-molding machines
simultaneously and the diversity of products
was astonishing. When polypropylene was
developed in 1963, Bachmann became a

major producer of combs, the product that had propelled the firm's initial growth a century earlier. In a sense, the company had come full circle.

In the 1970s, Bachmann Industries once again diversified into new fields, including model railroading, toy road racing sets, gun-cleaning kits, and holders and mailing cases for tape cassettes.

The growing field of model railroading included HO scale model trains and railway scenery products such as grass mats, miniature trees, and simulated mountains. Model railroading was growing as a hobby and Bachmann became a leader in supplying train equipment, scenery and scale-model buildings for railway villages.

Meanwhile, a Hong Kong firm, Kader Industrial, Ltd., had been established in 1948 to manufacture models and toys for export around the world and produced the enormously popular Cabbage Patch doll. Kader made the first model trains for Bachmann's American market in 1969 and this relationship grew until Kader acquired Bachmann Industries in its entirety in 1981.

In 1989, Kader, which also produces model railway equipment for other model brands, established Bachmann Industries (Europe). The initial product range, called Branchline, consisted of molds used to produce the Mainline range of railway models.

In 1992, Bachmann Industries (Europe) purchased the continental manufacturer Liliput and a German sales office was established to handle marketing, sales and product development for the Liliput brand.

Another acquisition came in 2000 when Bachmann Europe PLC purchased the British "N"-scale model manufacturer Graham Farish.

Kader Industrial, Ltd. is now, by volume, the largest manufacturer of model railways in the world. The Kader Group produces model trains for the whole world, providing the discerning model railway enthusiast true-to-life and true-to-scale models, which reproduce, in miniature, the realism of railways from yesterday and today.

Bachmann's E-Z Track® integrated track and roadbed system, introduced in 1994, is credited with revolutionizing the model-railroading hobby by making layouts more realistic and easier to build.

Bachmann acquired the assets of Williams Electric Trains in 2007 to extend their product line into the O gauge three-rail market. With the addition of three-rail models, Bachmann became the only railroading company to produce models for all popular hobby and train collector scales.

The quality of Bachmann products has been recognized by *Model Railroader Magazine*, which chose a Bachmann product as the finest in the industry for four successive years.

As Bachmann continues into its third century, it remains dedicated to the high quality products and management flexibility and imagination that have made it the worldwide leader in its field.

For additional information on Bachmann Industries, visit www.bachmanntrains.com and see what Bachmann Industries offers.

✧

Above: Toy and hobby lines were expanded to include high quality N scale electric trains.

Below: Plasticville® U.S.A. was first produced in 1947, with a variety of kits designed to enhance train layouts.

ELECTRON ENERGY CORPORATION

Electron Energy Corporation (EEC) is an international leader in the production of rare earth magnets and magnet assemblies. Privately owned, it was founded in 1970. The company began with just two employees working in an old milk house on a dairy farm near Manheim, Pennsylvania. From those humble beginnings, EEC progressed steadily to a position of prominence in high performance magnets of the type that are vital to various high-technology industries, including those of communications, defense, and medicine.

EEC's founder was Marlin S. Walmer (1929-1999), a pioneer in the science of rare earth magnets and their applications. An engineering graduate of Lehigh University, he subsequently received a Master of Science degree in physics from Franklin and Marshall College and, following two years of service in the U.S. Navy, began his professional career as a metallurgical engineer at the Hamilton Watch Company. While at Hamilton, Walmer developed a process to produce platinum cobalt magnets used in the world's first electric wristwatches. Although these magnets were very powerful, they were also very expensive—too expensive to find broad industrial application. Later, when an alloy system based on the rare earth element samarium and the transition metal element cobalt was discovered, which appeared to have potential for superior magnetic properties at far less cost, he left his position at Hamilton Watch to pursue the technical and commercial development of this revolutionary magnet material.

Actually, the so-called rare earth elements such as samarium and neodymium are neither rare nor earths. In fact, they are metals that occur in nature as oxides in relative abundance. Nevertheless, the term rare earth continues to be used for this family of metallic elements.

A rare earth permanent magnet is a combination of metals called an alloy—at least one of which is a rare earth—that retains its magnetism after being magnetized. Alloys based on rare earth elements are the latest and most advanced permanent magnets known today.

The first significant application of samarium cobalt magnets occurred in the defense industry in 1970 as part of advanced

technology used by the United States Air Force, and Walmer's fledgling company, EEC, was one of only three companies in the world that could produce them.

Commercial uses for rare earth magnets progressed steadily thereafter. In many industries the introduction of these materials was a revolutionary event as designers—stimulated by the advantages they offered of lighter weight and increased magnetic strength, stability, and temperature capability—pushed to create new devices and to reach higher levels of performance. Under Walmer's leadership, EEC focused on developing new alloys based on rare earths and on providing engineering and design expertise to enhance their customers' devices. From the outset, his business philosophy was straightforward: Be ethical. Produce high quality products for the most demanding applications. Delight the customer! Although Marlin Walmer died in 1999, he lived to see his forecast for the potential of rare earth magnets come to fruition. Walmer's pursuit of excellence and business philosophy continues at EEC under the leadership of his son, Michael H. Walmer, who is also an accomplished materials science engineer, and the excellent staff he recruited and trained.

The company's current home, a 40,000-square-foot facility in Landisville, Pennsylvania, was built in 1985 and is state-

of-the-art in equipment, expertise and technical personnel. As a fully-integrated producer, EEC designs alloys to meet specific requirements and then manufactures them under precisely controlled conditions, in effect, making each customer's order a custom product. That capability is now unique among U.S. magnet producers, as all others are processing magnets or alloys purchased from foreign sources.

Typically, EEC begins the design process by working closely with the customer to understand the requirements and to contribute know-how to the product's design. In this role

Electron Energy serves as a virtual in-house source of magnet technology and an extension of the customer's own technical capabilities.

The next step is to produce a magnet alloy that will meet the requirements. Manufacturing starts by combining the constituent elements and melting the alloy in vacuum furnaces. The alloy is then processed through a series of carefully controlled powder metallurgical procedures (pressing and sintering). Because sintered magnets are extremely hard and brittle, they cannot be brought to their final dimensions by conventional machining. Thus grinding, lapping and electrical discharge

Above: The enterprise that became EEC started in 1970 in a milk house in Lancaster County. From this very modest beginning the company grew steadily and in 1985 moved into a brand new facility of more than 40,000 square feet in Landisville, which is now their home. As a manufacturer of high technology products EEC's plant contains state-of-the-art equipment and a highly trained professional staff. The company is the only vertically-integrated magnet producer remaining in the U.S. In other words, EEC designs and then produces magnet alloys by melting them from constituent elements.

Left: Permanent magnets are alloys based on a combination of metallic elements that retain their magnetism after being magnetized. The most powerful magnets are made from the elements samarium and neodymium—rare earths. Actually, the rare earth family of elements is neither earths nor especially rare; rather, they are metals in common abundance. Because these magnet alloys are extremely hard, they require special handling and fabricating techniques. Typically, these magnets are manufactured by pressing and sintering powdered metal or by molding the particles in a polymer or metallic matrix. EEC produces both sintered and bonded magnets as well as magnet assemblies. The company specializes in applications engineering and in component design.

Specialized equipment is required in nearly every step of manufacturing high performance magnets. Typically, the alloy compositions are melted in a vacuum furnace, converted to powder and handled under protective atmospheres. Because they are extremely hard and brittle, rare earth magnets are finished by operations like grinding, lapping, and electrical discharge machining (EDM). Establishing and measuring magnetic properties also involves test equipment and procedures often unique to the industry. To design components and assemblies, EEC uses state-of-the-art computer techniques such as two- and three-dimensional finite element analysis.

cutting finishes them. Magnetizing requires specialized equipment, as do the procedures for testing and adjusting. Although the company's primary products are based on sintered samarium cobalt, they also offer neodymium-iron-boron and bonded magnets.

EEC's in-depth knowledge of magnetic materials and decades of practical experience with magnets and magnet assemblies enable it to provide innovative solutions to challenging customer requirements. Demand for EEC's technical services and application engineering capabilities has grown steadily. An engineering team is available to work closely with customers to determine their needs, participate in product design and ultimately fabricate prototypes. This, too, requires a professional staff and an investment in specialized equipment such as two- and three-dimensional finite element analysis computer-based modeling.

Quality products have been a hallmark of the company since its inception. EEC's quality system is certified to ISO 9001:2000; their traceability system has been approved by the aerospace industry. In support of their needs for magnetic materials characterization and for conducting research and development, EEC operates a state-of-the-art magnetics laboratory. Another distinctive attribute of Electron Energy is its commitment to being a technology leader—constantly pushing the edge of magnet technology. Research, often conducted in conjunction with universities and sponsored by various government agencies, has yielded a stream of new and improved products. Examples of successful research include:

- In response to a U.S. Air Force need for magnets that could maintain their properties at higher temperatures, EEC developed a composition capable of operating at 550 degrees Celsius and was awarded a U.S. patent. This proprietary alloy (SmCoUT™), which significantly increases the maximum service temperature of these powerful magnets, is also available for commercial applications.

- EEC developed a tougher, more crack-resistant version of neodymium-iron-boron (NEO) magnets. Typically, these magnets are quite brittle and EEC's new technology doubled the toughness of the magnet while maintaining very high magnetic properties. These new alloys have been patented and trademarked as "Tough NEO."

Such developments and others that have resulted from EEC's highly successful, ongoing research program play a large part in the reputation EEC enjoys.

The international profile of this small company is attested to by the important role its products and services play in many high-technology industries.

EEC is the world leader in supplying ready-to-assemble magnet stacks for traveling wave tubes, or TWTs, which are used to amplify microwave signals in communications and defense systems. Typical applications for these devices are the radars of F-16 and F-18 jets, unmanned aircraft and naval vessels. Modern satellites, both civilian and military, also rely on TWTs to communicate a wide range of functions. Other military applications of EEC magnets include reactor control system components in nuclear submarines and the gyroscopes and accelerometers used in control systems of air- and ground-based vehicles.

In addition to uses in satellite communication, EEC magnets provide the precision control, stability and reliability that are required of the accelerometers and gyroscopes of the space shuttle. Electron Energy's magnets also played a key role in the innovative propulsion system developed for NASA's Deep Space 1. EEC's high temperature samarium cobalt magnets were on board as Deep Space 1 exited our solar system, giving employees pride in being able to claim their products are "out of this world."

One of the newest and fastest-growing markets for rare earth magnets is medical science and technology. Examples include high-speed motors of hand-held, cordless surgical power tools.

The esteem in which Electron Energy Corporation's products and services are held is reflected in the many awards granted by customers and government agencies. The United States Small Business Administration has consistently recognized the company as Small Business Contractor of the Year in Region III and cited it for outstanding contributions and service to the nation. Customer recognition includes numerous certificates of excellence and citations for outstanding performance such as "consistently supplying superior products on time and at affordable cost." Following Marlin Walmer's death in 1999, a major producer of traveling wave tubes took the unusual step of presenting a memorial to EEC for "creating a lasting business relationship unparalleled by others." The International Rare Earth Magnets Society bestowed posthumous recognition on Walmer for a "lifetime of achievement" and the Chief Scientist of the U.S. Air Force wrote, "The Air Force and the nation have benefited greatly from his insight and energy. His contributions to our national defense and economy have been immense…we will miss him."

Proud of their heritage and of being an American company based in Pennsylvania, the management and employees view their past accomplishments as a solid base on which to build, and the principles established by the founder as guidelines for doing business, now and in the future. They are committed to maintaining Electron Energy Corporation's position as a world leader in advanced magnetic materials.

For more information about Electron Energy Corporation and its products and services, please visit www.electronenergy.com.

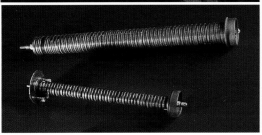

Applications for rare earth permanent magnets include almost every field of modern technology. In fact, in many cases, these magnets play a role in "modernizing" the technologies. Aerospace, telecommunications, and military systems are typical of those that use components enhanced by EEC products. One such component is traveling wave tubes, which are used to amplify microwave signals vital for satellite communications and electronic warfare. EEC is a world leader in supplying magnets for these devices.

IRONTON TELEPHONE COMPANY

The history of Ironton Telephone Company spans nearly the entire history of the telephone itself.

The company was formed by six local businessmen in 1909, only thirty-three years after Alexander Graham Bell completed the first successful telephone call. The new company was called the Ironton Rural Telephone Lines and provided telephone service for a rural farming area north of Allentown.

The company founders, unable to secure phone service from the companies serving Allentown, chose to build their own single pair of wires to the outer limits of Allentown, where they connected to the Lehigh Telephone Company.

In the early days, service was provided via 'crank' telephones, also known as magneto telephones. The operation continued until 1927, growing to a total of fifty-four subscribers. Meanwhile, attrition had dropped the number of original partners from six to two and they were struggling to keep the small, rural telephone company alive.

The owners were about ready to call it quits and abandon the service in favor of the Bell Company in Allentown when local businessman William D. George entered the picture. George needed economical telecommunication services to stay in contact with his meat markets in Allentown and Bethlehem and agreed to purchase a half interest in the faltering company. A few months later George traded a few building lots near Allentown for full ownership of the company.

George, aided by his son, Allen, operated the telephone company in conjunction with his meat packing and farming operations throughout the 1930s. A devastating storm in 1937 caused an ice build-up on the flimsy telephone wires strung between poles and resulted in severe damage to the system. Undaunted, George replaced the lines and rebuilt his small company.

The company grew to about 150 customers until expansion was halted during World War II and all available telephone equipment was put into the war effort. The company was beginning to grow again after the war when nature intervened once again.

On January 1, 1948, the most devastating ice storm on record hit the Lehigh Valley and telephone poles and lines littered streets throughout the region. Once again, the Georges rose to the occasion, rebuilt the facilities, and restored service to all subscribers within three months. The company had the foresight to purchase three miles of cable the year before, so when the storm hit, the new cable was installed with the help of Bell Telephone.

In addition, six miles of insulated wire was hung on fence posts from Mechanicsville through Ruchsville and Ironton, into Ballietsville and across the back roads to Schnecksville. Business customers were given priority. Phone service was restored as quickly as possible but, for a time, thirty businesses were forced to share a single telephone line.

In the early 1950s, the Bell Telephone Company in Allentown notified the Georges that the magneto facilities in Allentown would be eliminated in favor of new dial service. The Georges met this new challenge by investing the funds needed to replace the old-fashioned crank phones with the more modern dial phones. This project, supervised by Allen George, was completed in 1952, right on schedule.

The company grew slowly in subscriber numbers during the post-war era and during

the Korean conflict. By this time, William's grandson, William, II, known as Bill, had graduated from Parkland High School, earned a degree from Lehigh University, and joined the family firm.

Bill developed the idea of incorporating the telephone business, which until then had operated as a simple individual proprietorship. This was accomplished in September 1958 upon the receipt of a Letters Patent signed by then Governor George M. Leader. At this time, the company's name was changed to Ironton Telephone Company. Ironton was finally a full-fledged independent telephone company.

Bill also felt that this small, independent telephone company could better service its subscribers if it had its own switching system. At this time, Ironton Telephone owned only the outside plant and subscriber's telephones. The Bell Company maintained a switching center in downtown Allentown, connecting to Ironton's lines just outside the city limits.

An engineer was hired and plans were formulated to build a building, update and expand the outside cables, and build a switching system in the new building. To finance the expansion, a $360,000 loan was secured from the Rural

Electrification Administration, a division of the United States Department of Agriculture in Washington, D.C. To learn more about switching, Bill attended a switching system school at North Electric in Galion, Ohio, for six weeks. North Electric had been the successful bidder for a small 360-line switch as specified by Ironton's engineer.

At 2:01 a.m. on the foggy night of January 7, 1962, Ironton became a fully independent telephone company for the first time in its fifty-three year history when it cut over a relatively new switching system based on relays and a crossbar switch. At the time, Ironton Telephone had 612 subscribers, all on ten-party lines. This would quickly change, as many subscribers were waiting for one- and two-party service, heretofore unavailable.

In 1966, Ironton installed 'touch-tone' service, and the Ironton area became the first in the Lehigh Valley to have this type of modern service.

The crossbar switching system served Ironton well for about ten years, growing to 900 lines by 1971, the maximum configuration of the switch as originally specified. However, expanding the switch to meet the growth of the area was proven not to

✧

Above: Bill and Shirley Geeorge.

Below: Hattie and William George, circa 1960.

be feasible and it was determined that Ironton should replace the crossbar switch.

Bids were secured as required by the Rural Electrification Agency (REA) and Stromberg Carlson was low bidder with an electronic switch, known as the ESC-1. Again, Ironton was on the cutting edge of technology, this time the electronic age. A 2,000-square-foot addition was added to the building to house the new equipment and in July 1972, Ironton became the first company in the country to place the Stromberg 2,000-line analog electronic switch into service.

This new equipment, however, soon proved to be inadequate because it was economically incapable of providing such special services as call waiting and conference calling. In 1980, it was out for bid again, the third time in less than twenty years. This time the successful bidder was TRW Vidar and Ironton was on the cutting edge once again, this time the digital era. The new switch was co-located in the same room with the analog-electronic Stromberg switch.

Later in 1993, upon the advent of Equal Access, Ironton decided that it was time to form a long distance carrier to provide its own long distance service for its subscribers. So, Ironton Long Distance (ILD) was born.

By 1995, due to increased growth from the many new housing developments springing up throughout its service area, it was time to add to or replace the two switches. Ironton selected a digital Nortel DMS-100 switch to take it into the next century. The latest switch currently serves more than 17,000 access lines as of December 2007.

In 1994, Ironton entered into a partnership arrangement with a fledgling Internet Service Provider (ISP) called PenTeleData, a subsidiary of Pencor Services. Pencor also owns the Palmerton Telephone Company, a sister ILEC. The move meant Ironton was now entering the Internet era. PTD has developed a vast network of fiber optic cable in northeastern Pennsylvania and now serves more than 100,000 Internet customers. Ironton also provides broadband services to its subscribers utilizing DSL (digital service line) and modems.

In 1996, Ironton entered into yet another partnership with the local cable television provider, Service Electric Cable TV. The new partnership is called Service Electric Telephone (SET). Ironton provides the dial tone via its digital switch, and also customer service operations. Service's fiber-optic network throughout Lehigh and Northampton Counties and, ultimately, Phillipsburg, New Jersey is utilized to provide telephone service to the end-user.

By 1998, Ironton's management realized that it would need to expand its business office in order to accommodate the personnel growth in the Customer Service Department. An architect was retained, and a 22,000-square-foot building addition was designed. It would house not only the expanded CSR Division, but also the growing PBX Division. Additional garage space and storage for materials and supplied was also incorporated in the design. Move-in day was January 2, 2000.

In 2007, Ironton partnered with yet another cable television company, Service Electric Cablevision, to provide Voice Over Internet Protocol (VOIP) telephone service to a much wider area of eastern Pennsylvania. Again, Ironton is on the cutting edge of technology. Will there be more partnerships in the future? Only time will tell.

✧

Above: Ironton Telephone Company aerial view, circa 1975.

Below: Ironton Telephone Company's head-quarters building, circa 2001.

While Bill George, the company president since 1995, has spearheaded much of the company's progress since 1958, the firm is very much a family activity, with four of Bill's brothers and sisters currently involved. Allen M. M. George, Jr., serves as corporate vice president and director of operations; Patricia L. Stewart is secretary-treasurer, business office manager, and director of finance; Carolyn M. George is a customer service representative; and Rose M. Beck is a receptionist and a customer service representative. In addition, Bill's two stepsons, Michael and Ricky Harring, are also employed in the business; Michael as inventory manager and Ricky as a construction supervisor. Ironton's total employment now stands at fifty employees.

Today, nearly a century after it was founded as a small rural telephone system in 1909, Ironton Telephone Company is a Local Exchange Carrier providing local and long distance telephone service to residences and businesses in a seventeen square mile area of Lehigh County. Ironton also sells Nortell business telephone systems to small and medium size businesses throughout eastern Pennsylvania. Nephew David A. George heads up the sales department, selling both small and medium sized telephone systems and Internet broadband service to businesses in the Greater Lehigh Valley community.

Among Ironton's largest customers are the Lehigh Carbon Community College in Schnecksville; the Lehigh Career & Technical Institution, a vocational high school for students from Lehigh County's high schools; and the KidsPeace Hospital and complex for kids in crisis, also located near Schnecksville.

The Ironton Telephone Company's business philosophy is well stated in its Mission Statement, which reads: "Ironton Telephone Company's business existence is based on talented employees contributing loyal dedication and constant energy to provide its customers with the best quality of products at the best price with the best service. Its customers, both current and new, are interested in effective and efficient communications to meet their distinct objectives. Our company will work in tandem with our customers to identify a solution to their telecommunication necessities and desires. Therefore, based on our 'past' accomplishments and 'present' missions of continuing to perform to our best every day, our visions are what the 'future' holds because we perform our missions exceedingly well."

✧

Switching equipment.

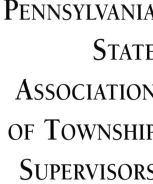
In the early days of the American Republic, as the fledgling nation's leaders struggled to create a truly representative government, Thomas Jefferson believed it was vital for each state to be portioned into wards, or townships, that would address the day-to-day concerns of its citizens. "Townships," he proclaimed, "have proved themselves the wisest invention ever devised by the wit of man for the perfect exercise of self-government." To this day, townships in the Commonwealth of Pennsylvania remain committed to that vision of government close to the people.

Pennsylvania's townships range in population from fewer than 100 people to more than 50,000 and provide a host of services to their residents, from road maintenance to sewage to parks and recreation. Since 1921, the Pennsylvania State Association of Township Supervisors has paved the way for township officials to provide those services in the most efficient, cost-effective, and accessible manner possible.

PSATS represents the elected and appointed officials of Pennsylvania's 1,456 townships of the second class, offering information, training and networking opportunities, and representation before the state legislature for some 10,000 local officials. As the needs and concerns of Pennsylvania's townships have grown over the years, PSATS has grown as well to fulfill those needs.

The history of townships in Pennsylvania is as old as the commonwealth itself. William Penn began establishing townships in "Penn's Woods" as early as 1683, but the concept was even older, arriving in the New World with the pilgrims. In fact, townships are the oldest form of organized government in the United States.

Penn's original townships were small, consisting of about ten families, but as the Industrial Revolution and westward migration brought increased development to the commonwealth, townships grew in size and number, along with cities and boroughs in Pennsylvania. Today, Pennsylvania's townships are home to 5.4 million residents, or forty-four percent of the state's population.

That development in the state's early years posed a threat to townships, however. As cities and boroughs grew, they often annexed developed portions of surrounding townships to increase their tax base. In 1899, the legislature stepped in and helped halt the annexation by providing for two categories of townships— first and second class. All townships with a population greater than 300 people per square mile were designated first class. Although the new classifications gave townships of the first class greater power when dealing with the impact of development, it would be more than 30 years before townships of the second class were granted those same powers.

Initially, a township's greatest, and very often, only responsibility was to maintain the roads. "Road supervisors" kept an eye on their municipality's thoroughfares and made sure they remained passable. Road equipment usually consisted of a wooden framework that a team of horses could drag over rough roads to smooth out the mud and ruts.

In 1913, an act of the state legislature created the Bureau of Township Highways within the State Highway Department, the predecessor to the Department of Transportation. The act placed general supervision of roads in the hands of three elected township supervisors, who could hire a road superintendent to oversee the construction and maintenance of roads for the entire township or several roadmasters to take charge of road maintenance in specific districts within the township.

The advent of the automobile brought new importance to the responsibility of road maintenance. Forward-thinking township supervisors and state officials, envisioning a future of increasing mechanization and development, realized that for townships to be able to secure their rights before the state legislature, they needed a united voice.

✧

The Pennsylvania State Association of Township Supervisors, located in Enola, near Harrisburg, the state capital, has been serving Pennsylvania's 1,456 townships of the second class since its creation by the General Assembly in 1921.

COURTESY OF SOCOLOW PHOTOGRAPHY.

Several county associations of township officials carried the idea of a statewide organization that would champion township government to the state capitol in Harrisburg. With the help of Joseph "Uncle Joe" Hunter, township commissioner of the State Highway Department, his assistant H. A. "Cappy" Thomson, and Representative Fred T. Gelder, a bill authorizing the formation of a state organization reached the desk of Governor William Sproul, who signed Act 189 into law on May 5, 1921. The Pennsylvania State Association of Township Supervisors was born.

Over the ensuing years, townships have changed tremendously, evolving from communities where farmers pitched in to tend to local roads to predominantly suburban landscapes run by men and women of all backgrounds whose main concern is no longer limited to road construction and maintenance.

As townships' needs grew, PSATS grew right along with them, offering more services to help township officials better meet the needs of their constituents. From its first years as a relatively inactive wing of the State Highway Department, PSATS has grown into the largest and most influential municipal association in the commonwealth. Under the leadership of a thirteen-member executive board and directors, beginning with Secretary Cappy Thomson in 1927 and continuing through Secretary Milton W. Delancey (1962-1976), Executive Director B. Kenneth Greider (1976-2000), and now Executive Director R. Keith Hite, PSATS has played a major role in helping shape township government into what it is today.

The days of township supervisors being concerned almost exclusively with the roads are long gone. The board of supervisors serves as the township's legislative body, setting policy, enacting local ordinances, adopting budgets, and levying taxes. It also fulfills the municipality's executive functions, enforcing ordinances, approving expenditures, and hiring employees.

While road-related issues are still a large part of the supervisors' responsibilities—townships maintain more than 51,000 miles of Pennsylvania's 118,000 miles of public roads—supervisors now play a greater role in providing new services and facilities for township residents. Among other things, they may establish a police force; provide for fire protection

and emergency services; organize planning commissions; adopt building, zoning, housing, and parking regulations; provide street lighting; construct and maintain sewage systems; provide and operate parks, playgrounds and other recreation facilities; and develop local emergency management and disaster preparedness plans.

PSATS provides a host of services to help supervisors meet township residents' needs efficiently and cost-effectively. Hite says PSATS has a dual identity: as a member-service organization and as an information clearinghouse.

The primary reason PSATS was created was to give townships a united voice in the state capital. Over the years, the Association has played a major role in shaping the laws that have laid the foundation for township government, from making sure townships receive their fair share of

✧

From its earliest days as an offshoot of the state Department of Highways, PSATS has helped townships address road-related issues such as construction, maintenance, and snow removal, which remain a primary responsibility for townships today.

the state's gasoline tax for road improvements to protecting townships from forced annexation and mergers.

PSATS keeps members informed about proposed legislation that affects townships and encourages township officials to voice their opinions to their state legislators. When important legislation is pending, PSATS notifies its members through the *PSATS Alert* bulletin and online discussion groups.

To enhance the Association's legislative efforts in Harrisburg, PSATS has developed a grassroots lobbying network consisting of its Legislative Committee, county legislative liaisons, and Association members.

Townships also need representation at the federal level, so PSATS works with the National Association of Towns and Townships to lobby on behalf of townships in Washington, D.C. PSATS was a founding member of this organization in 1976.

PSATS' flagship communication tool is its award-winning monthly magazine, the *Pennsylvania Township News*. Cappy Thomson started the publication in 1948, when the only reference available to township supervisors was the *Road Builder*, an independent newsletter from western Pennsylvania.

Initially, the *News* addressed such topics as roads, equipment purchasing, legislation, and township happenings. The first subscribers requested a page of questions and answers about township problems, and that column remains one of the magazine's most popular features to this day.

Over the years, the *News* has continued to address those initial topics, as well as newer issues facing township officials, from land use and environmental subjects to technological trends and alternative energy. Regular departments tackle such subjects as new and pending legislation and court decisions that affect townships; finances and personnel management; upcoming training, events, and deadlines; and township success stories.

Between issues of the *News*, the Association sends out the monthly *PSATS News Bulletin* to keep its members apprised of the most current happenings on Capitol Hill and other issues.

As PSATS entered the information age, it recognized the need to provide information to its members in the new realm of cyberspace and developed a Web site, located at www.psats.org. In addition to information on Association programs and services, the site also offers updates on relevant legislation; a searchable database of township ordinances; the entire text of the Second Class Township Code; a list of upcoming training opportunities; and a Local Government Marketplace, which provides information on suppliers of municipal products and services.

As townships' responsibilities grew more complex, PSATS stepped up to help township officials meet new challenges. The Association, under contract to several state agencies, offers an array of training opportunities to keep local officials educated on emerging issues and state requirements.

As part of the Pennsylvania Local Government Training Partnership, which includes many of the state's local government associations, PSATS coordinates more than 600 workshops across the state each year on topics ranging from road maintenance and storm water management to budgeting and bookkeeping.

PSATS also manages the Sewage Enforcement Officer Training Program, which prepares candidates to work for a local agency that permits onlot sewage disposal systems, and the Pennsylvania Construction Codes Academy, which prepares construction code officials for state certification exams and serves as a clearinghouse for township officials who need up-to-date information about the statewide building code.

PSATS also works with the state Department of Transportation to provide training, technical

✧

PSATS' Annual State Convention each April attracts nearly 5,000 township officials to Hershey for four days of conducting Association business, training, and networking. In 2004, U.S. President George W. Bush was the keynote speaker. This annual event is the largest municipal convention and trade show in the commonwealth.

assistance, and information about road products, techniques, and innovations through the Local Technical Assistance Program, or LTAP.

One of the Association's greatest education tools, by far, is its Annual State Convention and Trade Show, which has been held every year since 1921. This four-day event each April attracts nearly 5,000 township officials, employees, and guests to Hershey, Pennsylvania, for workshops, inspirational speakers, networking opportunities, and the state's largest municipal trade show. Featured speakers over the years have ranged from the president and vice president of the United States to governors, federal and state legislative leaders, and cabinet officers. Delegates to the convention also conduct Association business, electing officers and adopting resolutions to set Association policy for the coming year.

Over the years, PSATS has added other programs and services to meet the growing needs of its members. The Association has provided township officials, employees, and their families with quality health, life, and other insurance at a competitive rate through the Trustees Insurance Fund since 1959. PSATS' Unemployment Compensation Group Trust Fund offers townships unemployment compensation coverage at an affordable rate.

Through the Township Legal Defense Partnership, the Association supports townships in the legal arena. When a member township becomes involved in an appellate-level case with statewide implications, PSATS may direct its legal counsel to file a friend-of-the-court brief on behalf of the township and help the township's solicitor during the adjudication process.

PSATS also offers membership in three auxiliary associations for the professionals and volunteers that townships depend on for their specific expertise. The Pennsylvania State Association of Township Engineers provides seminars, networking opportunities, a quarterly newsletter, and technical resources to municipal engineers. The Township Planning Association provides planning commissions, zoning hearing boards, and township supervisors with the training, technical assistance, and information they need to navigate the increasingly complex world of land use planning. The Pennsylvania State Association of Township Solicitors provides training opportu-

nities, a bimonthly newsletter, and other services to municipal attorneys.

PSATS also helps townships fulfill the state mandate of random drug and alcohol testing of township employees who have a commercial driver's license. The CDL Program coordinates testing opportunities and uses computer software to randomly select employees for testing.

As it has done since its creation in the early twentieth century, the Pennsylvania State Association of Township Supervisors will continue to expand its programs and services to meet the changing needs of its member townships.

"PSATS has always been a dynamic and fluid organization," Hite says. "It is ever vigilant in looking for ways to provide township officials with the tools they need to best serve their communities."

Nearly 50 years after Thomas Jefferson described townships as man's "wisest invention" for the exercise of self-government, Abraham Lincoln, in his famous Gettysburg address, expressed hope for the continuation of government "of the people, by the people, [and] for the people." Nothing better embodies Jefferson's conviction and Lincoln's vision of a government close to the people than Pennsylvania's townships of the second class.

As the concerns and issues facing township officials in Pennsylvania increase, PSATS will be there to help them face new challenges, meet their communities' needs, and keep township government strong well into the future.

✧

Through the many training programs it administers in conjunction with the Governor's Center for Local Government Services and other state agencies, PSATS provides opportunities for local government officials and employees from across the commonwealth to learn from qualified instructors and each other.
COURTESY OF SOCOLOW PHOTOGRAPHY.

Highmark Blue Shield

As one of Pennsylvania's leading health insurers, Highmark Blue Shield has been helping its members live longer, healthier lives for nearly seventy years by ensuring access to affordable, high quality health insurance and services.

As consumers begin to take a more active role in their healthcare, Highmark Blue Shield offers the widest range of products, access to all area hospitals and the most responsive customer service.

Through growth in services, healthcare options and state-of-the-art technologies, Highmark Blue Shield remains true to its mission. And, it is continually developing new information sources designed to help consumers make more informed decisions about health benefits and their personal health.

Through the Health Excellence Partners program, Highmark Blue Shield has built a comprehensive system that allows physicians and patients to share information about health issues more freely. This program coordinates data on disease prevention, risk assessment, physician contact, and utilization by patients and encourages interaction with health coaches and other sources to facilitate timely interventions on health issues.

By using health risk assessments, Highmark Blue Shield has worked to better manage chronic conditions and help members live longer, healthier lives. Employers value this effort, realizing that prevention and wellness contribute significantly toward managing healthcare costs.

For a number of years, Hallmark Blue Shield has offered Blues On Call™, a comprehensive approach to total patient care. This service provides members with answers to everyday health-related questions and assistance with health discussions they have with their medical providers, as well as more extensive ongoing help with chronic illnesses through a toll-free, twenty-four hour helpline staffed by registered nurses.

In 2006, Highmark Blue Shield introduced a new tool to help employers manage costs while encouraging appropriate care. Through a special unit of nurses, registered dietitians and exercise physiologists, Blues On Call Plus offers tailored programs that meet customers'

unique needs. Blues On Call Plus addresses the range of healthcare services with an increased emphasis on wellness and preventive care to help prevent diseases before they become chronic conditions. As part of the program, Highmark Blue Shield provides medical directors and physician consultants to help resolve health-related conditions that impact productivity.

Highmark Blue Shield members may view and manage their own healthcare information through Personal Health Record, a private, secure, and password-protected Web-based tool. As a single source of health information for members and their dependants, the Personal Health Record utilizes medical claims and administrative information as well as information that is entered by consumers themselves.

The Personal Health Record provides members with a personalized Health Action Plan that gives specific action items for health improvements, links to programs to manage possible health issues, and detailed information about health conditions to ensure that members are fully educated about their health and have options to make improvements. Members who are identified with diabetes, asthma, coronary artery disease, or more than thirty other health topics are given access to a condition manager that provides specific programs, tools and information to take the necessary health actions and better understand their conditions.

Lifestyle Returns, the Highmark Blue Shield program offering incentives to members to take five simple steps to gauge and address their health conditions, continues to evolve and expand. Member companies adopting the program have reported that a number of individuals discovered chronic conditions and potentially life-threatening situations through Lifestyle Returns. Such is the case with Highmark Blue Shield itself, where employee participation in Lifestyle Returns has grown from 9 percent in 2005 to 50 percent in 2006.

Members enrolled in Highmark Blue Shield's high-deductible health plans doubled to nearly 42,000 in 2006. About half those members subscribed to Health Savings Accounts (HSAs). This is encouraging news since the preliminary findings of a Highmark Blue Shield study revealed that HSA account holders make a positive change in their use of healthcare service.

Although Highmark is headquartered in Pittsburgh, the company employs more than 5,000 individuals in central Pennsylvania and the Lehigh Valley. Highmark exerts an enormous economic impact in the communities it serves throughout Pennsylvania. A recent study shows that the organization's corporate-wide positive impact exceeds $2.5 billion.

Highmark supports the community and its employees in a variety of ways. In 2006, for example, the company contributed more than $240 million across Pennsylvania to strengthen the communities where it does business and its employees call home.

Event sponsorships in Central and Eastern Pennsylvania are far-reaching and include support of nonprofit community events, health and wellness oriented programs, and the arts and cultural activities throughout its service area. And, Highmark employees log an estimated 22,000 hours of volunteer service annually to a variety of community-based organizations and donate more than $1 million to the United Way across its service.

Highmark Blue Shield is an independent licensee of the Blue Cross and Blue Shield Association, an association of independent Blue Cross and Blue Shield Plans. For more information, visit www.highmark.com.

✧

SHARING THE HERITAGE

HIGHMARK

The history of Highmark, Inc., begins during the Great Depression of the 1930s and the genesis of the Blue Plan movement. To ensure the availability of funds to pay for hospital and medical services, respectively, the hospital association based in Pittsburgh sponsored the formation of the organization later known as the Blue Plan of Western Pennsylvania and the Pennsylvania Medical Society backed the founding of Pennsylvania Blue Shield. In 1996, Highmark was formed through the merger of those two Blue Plans.

These were unique organizations from the outset—nonprofit corporations that were structured along traditional business lines. Without shareholders to keep satisfied, margins were held in reserve, applied to subsidize the cost of coverage for poor health risks or reinvested in the business. To this day, this represents an important distinction between Highmark and for-profit competitors when it comes to shouldering the risk of underwriting healthcare coverage programs for at-risk populations. While such programs are designed to break even financially, they typically lose money.

As independent organizations from the mid-1930s to the mid-1990s, the Blue Plan of Western Pennsylvania and Pennsylvania Blue Shield introduced an unbroken string of innovations that helped to ensure access to healthcare services for the widest possible cross-section of the community.

These included:
- First prepaid program of healthcare coverage;
- First program of health benefits for persons not covered by a group plan;
- Establishing health benefits as a collective bargaining issue;
- Developing the first uniform nationwide program of coverage;
- Dedicated program for seniors (predating Medicare);
- First program of health benefits for the unemployed;
- First program of health benefits for the working poor; and,
- First program of health benefits for children of the working poor.

In the first decade since its founding, Highmark has refined its mission and its strategies to reflect evolving community and business needs, but the central themes remain the same—ensuring access to affordable healthcare coverage for the widest possible cross section of the community and helping people live longer and healthier lives. In one way or another, everything Highmark does ties back to these overarching goals. Highmark remains deeply committed to the communities in which it does business, and where its 18,500 employees live and work.

The company also is deeply committed not just to remaining financially stable, but doing all it can to be a growing, socially responsible organization. Because Highmark competes with for-profit health insurers, many of whom are headquartered outside of Pennsylvania and who enter and leave the market as the underwriting winds shift to maximize the return on their shareholders' investments, Highmark must remain financially competitive in order to fulfill its mission for the benefit of members and the communities it serves.

Highmark remains the preeminent health insurer in Pennsylvania, with the largest market share in the private business segment and a significant role in the administration of public health programs for the federal and state governments. Operating on an unmatched scale, the company leverages its influence for the benefit of the communities it serves. Its impact on the economy and quality of life in the Commonwealth is felt in many ways that extend beyond the role of an underwriter of health benefits programs.

For example, Highmark in 2006 contributed more than $200 million to Pennsylvania hospitals, human-services agencies, schools, community organizations and arts and cultural groups. In addition, Highmark supports and administers CHIP and adultBasic, two statewide public programs serving Pennsylvanians who otherwise lack access to healthcare coverage. The Caring Foundation, a Highmark affiliate and innovation, has provided coverage for more than

Highmark has Web-based programs that enable customers to enroll in and modify their benefit programs online, check the status of claims and obtain medical counseling and wellness information.

680,000 uninsured children and adults since its founding some twenty years ago.

Highmark has Web-based programs that enable customers to enroll in and modify their benefit programs online, check the status of claims and obtain medical counseling and wellness information.

Moreover, Highmark pays substantial taxes despite its not-for-profit status. In 2006, it paid more than $233.7 million in federal, state and municipal taxes.

Highmark's impact on the Commonwealth exceeds $2 billion annually, including $1 billion in the Western Region counties and nearly $500 million in Central Pennsylvania. To place this in perspective, $2 billion exceeds the impact of all of Pennsylvania's professional sports teams combined, all of Pennsylvania's arts and cultural organizations combined and the impact of tourism on the Pittsburgh area. It has twice the projected impact of the ten gaming facilities currently contemplated in the state.

Moving forward, Highmark is calling upon its seven decades of innovation and unmatched experience to design programs that address the evolving healthcare needs of Pennsylvanians. In doing so, the company is blending its healthcare expertise with leading edge technological advancements in the fields of information management, e-commerce and communications.

Highmark was the first health insurer in the nation to introduce Web-based programs that enable customers to enroll in and modify

their benefit programs online, check the status of claims and obtain medical counseling and wellness information.

A new generation of Highmark products addresses the need to control costs by increasing incentives for customers to take a greater hand in their health. These new products include tax-advantaged health savings accounts, health reimbursement accounts and flexible spending accounts that encourage individual members to become more proactive in managing their health.

Highmark's Pennsylvania-bred heritage is central to its identity and the corporation is committed to growing its presence in the Commonwealth in the decades ahead.

In 2005, Highmark opened a world-class data processing facility in Central Pennsylvania that will enable it to import work from outside the state in addition to supporting its future business needs. And unlike some of its competitors, Highmark has kept all of its customer-service functions within the borders of Pennsylvania—nothing has been outsourced to other states or countries.

Highmark recognizes that its strengths are largely derived from the character of the people of Pennsylvania who have supported the enterprise since the 1930s and it aims to remain a strong and vital force in the state throughout the twenty-first century.

Highmark is based in Pittsburgh, Pennsylvania and on the Internet at www.highmark.com.

✧

Highmark strongly believes in supporting the communities it serves. In 2006, Highmark contributed millions to Pennsylvania hospitals, human-services agencies, schools, community organizations and cultural groups.

ELITE SPORTSWEAR L.P.

Located in the heart of Reading, Pennsylvania, Elite Sportswear is the world's leading manufacturer of gymnastics apparel. Elite Sportswear, L.P., has been part of the Reading community since it was founded in 1981. The company's brand name, GK, is recognized around the world for superior quality, style and fit.

With so much manufacturing going off shore, Elite Sportswear is proud to be able to say 'made in America'! Everything from design to marketing to manufacturing and shipping is conducted under one roof in the Reading facility. The company celebrated its twenty-fifth anniversary in 2006, and today, the company that started with thirty-five employees, boasts a workforce of over 300.

Elite Sportswear's main product line has always been gymnastics apparel. This unique market demands quality and attention to service. The challenging market is a perfect fit for Elite, a company that thrives on quality, service and challenges. Although gymnastics has been the main market for GK, the same quality and service have also been applied to the other markets that GK serves. Figure skating, dance, cheer and track & field all receive the same GK treatment.

Elite's GK logo has been seen on most of the top American gymnasts as well as on many of the top gymnasts from around the world. From 1989 through 1992, Elite was the official apparel supplier of the U.S. National Team, the U.S. World Championship team and the 1992 U.S. Olympic team in

❖

Above: All around Olympic Gold Medalists Paul Hamm and Carly Patterson.

Below: Vitaly Scherbo on rings.

The Choice of Champions

Barcelona, Spain. Following the 1992 Olympics, rising star Shannon Miller agreed to endorse a line of gymnastics workout apparel for GK. The Shannon Miller Workout Collection continued for six years, during which time, Shannon achieved the status of the most decorated gymnast in U.S. history!

In addition to Shannon, GK products have been endorsed by Olympic medalists Amanda Borden, Jaycie Phelps, Amy Chow, Svetlana Boguinskaia, Lilia Podkopayeva and Carly Patterson and by World Championship medalists, Chellsie Memmel, Jana Bieger, Nastia Liukin and Shawn Johnson. Male endorsees have included Olympians John Roethlisberger, Chainey Umphrey, John Macready, Vitaly Scherbo, Rustam Sharipov, Blaine Wilson, Jason Gatson, Paul Hamm and Morgan Hamm.

Elite signed its first international contract with the Ukrainian Gymnastics Federation in 1993 when Elite became the official competitive supplier for the Ukrainian National, World Championship and Olympic teams. The relationship with Ukrainian gymnastics and their federation leader, Lyudmila Tourishcheva, the most decorated gymnast in the world, was extremely successful for both parties. In 1996, Elite outfitted the Ukrainian Olympic team and the GK logo was photographed repeatedly as it traveled to the awards stand five times,

including when Lilia Podkopayeva received her All Around Gold Medal, the most coveted of all of the gymnastics medals given at the Olympic games.

GK has had a number of international contracts in the past decade. In addition to the U.S. teams outfitted by Elite, GK has taken great pride in being the official apparel sponsor for the Ukraine, German, and Belarus National Teams, and the company is currently the official competitive apparel sponsor for the Australian National Team. Distributorships have been opened throughout Europe, and with seventeen distributors currently in place, sales have become such a worldwide occurrence that the GK website is available in six languages, in addition to English.

Meanwhile back in the United States, Elite was chosen by adidas to manufacture the competitive apparel for the U.S. National, World Championship and Olympic Teams, beginning with the 2000 Olympic team and continuing today. And even though the 2008 Australian Olympic team will be wearing apparel bearing an adidas logo, their apparel will be manufactured by GK for adidas.

Sponsoring these prestigious National, World Championship and Olympic teams has

brought great recognition to the GK product and to the attention it gives to quality and service. Additionally, by sponsoring such major events as Junior Olympic Nationals, the company has won the respect of many more gymnastics enthusiasts through their strong commitment to the young gymnasts who are the promise of tomorrow.

As the official apparel supplier to USA Gymnastics' Junior Olympic and Grassroots Development programs, the GK brand outfits the very important developmental youth teams and programs for all four disciplines of gymnastics. Programs such as Future Stars, TOPS and Jump Start Development all receive the benefit of Elite's special touch and dedication to contributing back to the sport.

Elite's commitment has not gone unnoticed by the gymnastics community. Elite Sportswear was awarded the Shirley Marshak Memorial Award for recognition of its contributions to the TOPs program, one of the developmental programs in place nationally. In her acceptance speech, the owner, president, and CEO of Elite Sportswear, Sallie Weaver, voiced a very GK view of the honor. "It seems odd to be given an award for doing something we enjoy doing so much," she said.

In recent years, GK has also become the first gymnastics apparel manufacturer to offer a special fit for athletes with disabilities. GK worked with special needs athletes, coaches, and clubs to develop a special fit for leotards and warm-ups that will live up to GK's superior reputation.

Above: Chellsie Memmell.

Below: Shannon Miller, most decorated gymnast in U.S. history.

According to Weaver, who was the driving force behind the new special fit, "Developing a special fit for athletes with disabilities has long been a dream of mine. The special needs gymnastics market is not a very large market, but it's a market that deserves to have gymnastics apparel that fits. These athletes have enough obstacles to overcome daily. Having to get a leotard that fits should not be one of them!"

As in all sports, gymnastics depends considerably on sponsorships from leaders in the industry to help the sport thrive and grow. Elite Sportswear GK is one of the most notable and most active supporters of the sport. During the twenty-six years Elite has manufactured GK apparel, the company has been a steady and dependable supporter of the sport at all levels. GK has always been there, ready to pull out all the stops and do

whatever was needed to meet the demands of the unique sport of gymnastics.

Elite also offers a line of figure skating apparel, which has earned the same reputation for quality and integrity as the gymnastics lines. When GK entered the figure skating market in 1995, one of the most recognizable names in figure skating, Olympic Gold medalist, Oksana Baiul, endorsed the very first line of GK skating apparel.

Following on the heels of the figure skating line, dance and cheer lines were introduced and have also been received with the same enthusiasm as Elite's other apparel.

In 2005, GK obtained the license to manufacture the Tousse line of track and field apparel, thus adding yet another sport to its list of fans. As with all the other markets, the Tousse line is manufactured entirely in the Reading facility, with the same care and expertise that GK brings to all its apparel.

As in any other business, there is little forward movement without large strides in technology. GK's website, www.gkelite.com, in addition to being multi-lingual, boasts the first interactive Design Studio, which allows its customers to create and view their own leotard and warm-up designs. With more than a dozen different catalogs produced annually, the website is a must in keeping GK's customers up to date and informed.

The commitment of this company can be summed up by the company Mission Statement, which is not just words on the wall, but the guiding force in all of Elite Sportswear's daily operations: "Our purpose is to be the athletes' first choice. We are committed to providing the ultimate in service, quality, selection, innovation, value and integrity."

The pride shared by all of Elite's employees guarantees that the tradition of excellence will continue as long as the GK logo is part of the sports they service.

✧

Shawn Johnson.

PENNSYLVANIA CHAMBER OF BUSINESS AND INDUSTRY

The Pennsylvania Chamber of Business and Industry is the Statewide Voice of Business in the Commonwealth.

Since its establishment as the State Chamber of Commerce in 1916, the Pennsylvania Chamber has adhered to its core mission of advancing the growth and prosperity of Pennsylvania businesses; and providing information and opportunities for involvement to its members regarding state government's legislative and regulatory activity.

As a member-driven organization, the Pennsylvania Chamber is on Capitol Hill in Harrisburg ensuring that the concerns of the business community are heard by state policymakers. Our highly visible and experienced team is dedicated to influencing public policy and developing key relationships with lawmakers; monitoring the bills and regulations that could affect businesses' bottom line; and presenting expert testimony before legislative committees considering proposed policy changes.

Through weekly, monthly and quarterly publications, members are kept up-to-date on the latest business-related news from the General Assembly. Members are also entitled to a wide variety of other benefits that include participation in events with government officials and money-saving group-buying programs through the Pennsylvania Chamber's Affinity Partner initiatives.

The Pennsylvania Chamber is a recognized leader in helping businesses understand and comply with complex state and federal workplace regulations. As such, the Pennsylvania Chamber offers numerous professional educational programs, including conferences and roundtables, as well as informative guide books, on a wide variety of issues important to the business community.

Based on the overwhelming needs of smaller businesses in the state, the Pennsylvania Chamber established an insurance subsidiary in the early 1990s. PCI Insurance, a wholly-owned subsidiary, offers the same healthcare plan and service options available to Fortune 500 companies. And Insurance Coalition, Inc., formed in 2005, provides a complete portfolio of unique employee benefit options for companies of all sizes across Pennsylvania.

Today, the Pennsylvania Chamber of Business and Industry is the largest broad-based business association in the Commonwealth, serving more than 24,000 members and customers throughout the state, and employing nearly fifty percent of the private work force.

In 1995 the Pennsylvania Chamber became one of only five state chambers in the nation at the time to be accredited by the U.S. Chamber of Commerce for meeting the highest standards of performance and effectiveness.

Through the years, the Pennsylvania Chamber of Business and Industry has taken bold action on behalf of its members to advance pro-growth, pro-jobs and pro-business policies, fostering the competitiveness of job creators and ensuring the long-term economic prosperity of the Commonwealth.

❖

The Pennsylvania Chamber's member-driven legislative agenda is at the heart of its mission to ensure the Commonwealth's economic vitality.

PENNSYLVANIA LUMBERMENS MUTUAL INSURANCE COMPANY

✧

Above: Chairman J. William Lee and President and CEO John K. Smith.

Below: One Commerce Square.

In the autumn of 1894, a group of lumber dealers and woodworkers from several eastern states met to discuss issues of mutual concern. Among the hottest topics were that of insurance coverage and the high rates being charged to members of their industries by stock insurance companies of the time.

It was at this meeting that one Philadelphia lumber dealer, Edward Henson, proposed a plan for these business owners and operators to form a mutual insurance company dedicated to meeting their unique insurance needs. Henson's ideas were positively received by the group, and the result was the establishment of Pennsylvania Lumberman's Mutual Fire Insurance Company on March 1, 1895.

In that first year alone, it was reported that insurance in force totaled $882,316. There were no losses, and assets were reported at $60,000 with liabilities of only $375.

Pennsylvania Lumbermens Mutual Insurance Company (PLM) passed the $1 million mark in net surplus in 1921, which represented a "launch point" for accelerating growth. The company grew the surplus to more than $2 million by the end of the decade, with assets swelling from $1.5 million to $2.6 million during the same period.

The company's staff grew along with its revenues. From a four-person crew housed in a single room on the second floor of Henson's company in 1895, PLM's workforce increased to a staff of nearly four times the original number by 1901. That year, the company moved to the Drexel Building in Philadelphia's financial district.

PLM's growth slowed somewhat during the slumping economy of the 1930s although assets continued to increase to $4.2 million during the decade. The death of Henson in 1931 was a traumatic time for the company but the appointment of Justin Peters as his successor helped smooth the transition. The Board of Directors also hired a number of insurance and financial professionals during this period, breaking the tradition of employing only managers with a background in the lumber business.

The need for lumber and building products slackened during the years of World War II, but during the post-war boom of the 1940s, PLM's assets more than doubled. The post-war building boom continued into the 1950s, sparking an era of unprecedented prosperity. Assets hit an all-time high of $16.2 million in 1955, with its surplus reaching nearly $8 million.

The company moved into a new office in 1956, occupying two floors of the former Ritz-Carlton Hotel in the center of Philadelphia. In recognition of its anchor tenant, the building

was renamed the Pennsylvania Lumbermens Mutual Insurance Building.

PLM's production increases continued into the early 1960s with a growing number of policies being written by the General Business Division, which had been reorganized in 1933. This division expanded with the establishment of branch offices in New York, North Carolina, Arizona and California.

Over the next few years, a series of natural disasters, particularly hurricanes, heavily impacted the General Business Division. The Lumber Division, however, continued to earn consistent profits. This prompted management to renew its commitment to PLM's core business—underwriting lumber, woodworking, and building material operations.

To emphasize the reestablishment of its core business, lumber manager J. Frank Braceland was named president in 1967. Under his leadership the company's surplus more than tripled between 1968 and 1978.

For most of its existence, PLM operated as part of a cooperative group—the Association Lumber Mutuals. In the 1980s, the cooperative group disbanded, turning former associates into competitors. PLM met this challenge by expanding the number of field representatives and moving beyond its traditional geographic borders. Headed by President C. A. Kane, PLM continued to grow throughout the 1980s. During this period the company headquarters moved back to Philadelphia's insurance district, taking up residence in the refurbished Curtis Center, once home of the *Saturday Evening Post*.

PLM entered the 1990s under the leadership of President J. William Lee. Under Lee, PLM repackaged many of its established lines, organized new coverages to fit the needs of a changing industry and moved into writing new categories of risk within the forest product industry.

An economic downturn in the insurance industry in the 1990s adversely impacted many of the specialty companies, leaving PLM as one of the few insurance specialists in the wood niche. This provided an opportunity for PLM to emerge as the premier provider of specialty insurance coverages for the lumber, woodworking, building material and allied industries.

PLM has increased its book of business by an average of twenty percent each year since 2000 with its assets and surplus reaching record highs. This growth has been led by John K. Smith, CPCU, who joined PLM in 1998 and was named president in 2003. Smith has capitalized on the company's gains by expanding field operations nationwide. The company has also further refined the risks it writes, concentrating on its core markets and offering a broader range of coverages. This has been supported with major improvements to the company's infrastructure and human resources.

PLM has always recognized its obligation and responsibilities to the communities in which it conducts business. The company's commitment to a community giving program continues in its relationship with the United Way, Pennsylvania Horticulture Society and Philadelphia Fire Museum.

In 2007, Pennsylvania Lumbermens Mutual Insurance Company moved to a new location in the center of Philadelphia at the One Commerce Square Building at 2005 Market Street.

❖

Above: Original staff on the second floor of Edward Henson's lumberyard, 921 North Front Street.

Below: Edward J. Henson, 1902.

CONESTOGA WOOD SPECIALTIES CORPORATION

Conestoga Wood Specialties Corporation began in 1964 in a rural area northwest of Philadelphia. Norman and Samuel Hahn formed the company in an effort to chart their own destiny by producing high-quality cabinet doors and drawer fronts.

Through their leadership, the company has grown from a two-car garage and $20,000 in sales their first year to eight manufacturing facilities and sales of wood doors and components exceeding $240 million in 2006.

Conestoga Wood Specialties is the premier supplier of wood doors and components for the kitchen, bath and furniture industries. The company, headquartered in East Earl, Pennsylvania sells its products to manufacturers in all fifty states and overseas.

Norman and Sam learned their woodworking skills in the mid- to late 1950s at the New Holland Planing Mill. They also worked evenings and weekends building and installing cabinets in the East Earl area. In 1960, Norman started his own company—Stylecraft Kitchens—with Sam as an employee.

Norman eventually sold his interest in Stylecraft and started Conestoga Wood Specialties in May 1964 with Sam. They knew from experience that cabinet doors and drawer fronts were the most difficult part of the cabinet to make, and they thought manufacturers would be willing to outsource that costly and time-consuming function.

The Hahns sold to several small cabinet shops in the area, and trained their sights on Marvel Kitchens, a company known to have extremely high expectations of their suppliers. Although advised that they would have a difficult time satisfying Marvel, Norman and Sam rightly assumed that if Marvel Kitchens began buying their products everyone else would too.

Marvel Kitchens initially rebuffed Norman and Sam's gestures because they doubted the brothers had the experience to produce the quality products to meet their demands. Despite repeated rejection, the Hahns didn't give up, and a year later Marvel Kitchens, impressed with Norman and Sam's persistence and product quality, agreed to a test order.

That led to many more orders and, as predicted, when news got out that Conestoga was producing cabinet doors for Marvel Kitchens, business boomed. They quickly had to find more space and in 1966 moved from the two-car garage to a new location across the street to what is now the corporate headquarters including the executive offices and a custom manufacturing plant.

The East Earl plant has been expanded several times through the years to include four separate manufacturing buildings and a brand new warehouse facility. As the company's sales grew, it became clear that to expand further it would have to purchase additional manufacturing plants in other parts of the country. The company purchased its first off-site plant in 1978 in Darlington, Maryland. It now owns additional plants in Jacksonville and Mountain View, Arkansas, Kenly, North Carolina, Beavertown and Beaver Springs, Pennsylvania and Tooele, Utah.

The company operates as three distinct business units:

- The Custom Division provides components to custom kitchen manufacturers, producing kitchen at a time quantities;
- The Contract/OEM Division sells large quantities of doors to high volume cabinet manufacturers; and
- Dimension Mills supplies wood panels and framing to the Custom and Contract Divisions to produce finished doors.

The company boasts well over one million square feet of manufacturing space and more than 2,200 employees nationally. Conestoga's Custom Division offers more than one hundred published door designs and hundreds more that are unpublished. The Custom and Contract Divisions offer nearly twenty standard wood species in multiple grades as well as several imported species.

❖

Above: Solid wood raised panel doors.

Below: Conestoga's first manufacturing facility.

The company has the ability to offer an extensive range of custom wood components, including doors, drawer fronts, beaded front frames, dovetail drawer boxes, moldings, ready-to-assemble cabinet systems, finishing, a variety of radius products, special designs components, rigid thermal foil doors and medium-density fiberboard products.

The manufacturing and support systems incorporate state-of-the-art technology and custom-designed equipment that enables Conestoga to meet its customers' specific needs. Conestoga also manages its own dimension mills to ensure the highest-quality wood standards throughout production.

Conestoga ensures prompt and safe delivery of products via Conestoga Wood Transportation, which delivers a large percentage of the company's raw materials and assembled components via its company-owned fleet of trucks. By using its own people and equipment, the company calls on its expertise in delivering fragile wooden cargo damage free, on time and at a lower price.

Currently, Conestoga is initiating growth plans, expanding its domestic manufacturing base to include the western portion of the United States. This will allow them to increase their level of service and gain additional market penetration throughout the west.

In its efforts to provide its customers with industry leading products, Conestoga utilizes state-of-the-art machinery and construction materials from around the world. On January 1, 2006, the company announced it had partnered with La Venus S.p.A. of Italy to form a joint venture named Impresa Technologies, LLC, producing doors made from a low-priced alternative to wood that is popular in Europe.

For more than four decades, Conestoga Wood Specialties has been a symbol of quality and innovation. The company, its people, and its products reflect the pride and tradition that speaks highly of the founders' Pennsylvania Dutch heritage. The company's unique combination of Old World Craftsmanship and cutting-edge technology allows Conestoga to set the standards by which excellence is measured.

Conestoga Wood Specialties is a learning organization dedicated to continuous improvement through employee involvement and teamwork. Guided by its Christian principles and corporate values of integrity, respect, accountability, resourcefulness and innovation, Conestoga will continue to offer customers the finest wood doors and components in the industry.

For additional information on Conestoga Wood, visit www.conestogawood.com on the Internet.

✧

Above: Conestoga's dovetail drawer boxes.

Bottom, left: Ready-to-assemble wood components.

Below: Presidential cathedral door.

YORKTOWNE CABINETRY

Yorktowne Cabinetry® is celebrating its one hundredth birthday with the slogan, "A Century of Craftsmanship, A Lifetime of Quality." The slogan well describes the semi-custom manufacturers' reputation for producing high quality cabinetry and accessories that are made-to-order, one kitchen at a time.

Yorktowne Cabinetry traces its beginnings to 1908 when Jacob Pechenik opened a factory in Brooklyn, New York to produce millwork wooden doors, window frames and sashes.

The company, then known as Colonial Products Company, manufactured custom kitchen cabinets for the New York City market. In the 1930s, the firm began manufacturing a diversified line of wood products, including Venetian blinds.

Pressures of the economic depression of the 1930s led Charles Pechenik, who had succeeded Jacob as head of the company, to close the Brooklyn plant and purchase the Dallastown Furniture Company. The company's equipment was loaded on a train and moved to Dallastown, Pennsylvania, where operations began in April 1937.

The company, now known as Colonial Products, contributed to the World War II mobilization effort by producing pre-fabricated footlockers for the United States Navy and medical corps equipment for military facilities around the world. Colonial Products was the first woodworking firm in York County to re-tool operations as part of the war effort.

The company resumed production of kitchen cabinets following the war and became an innovator when it introduced a Natural Birch finish in 1951. Prior to that, painted wood cabinets were the standard.

This reputation for innovation was further enhanced a year later when Charles began manufacturing Yorktowne Kitchens in quantity, then holding them in inventory for future delivery. Yorktowne Kitchens were nationally advertised and sold coast-to-coast.

As the popularity of Yorktowne Kitchens increased during the post-war building boom, Colonial Products introduced several new lines of kitchen cabinets, along with plastic

bathroom vanities and television cabinets. In addition, furniture for the kitchen and breakfast room were mass-produced and sold to furniture and department stores.

By the end of the 1950s, Colonial operated several manufacturing plants throughout York County, totaling more than 650,000 square feet. The growth included facilities in Red Lion, Milton, Mifflinburg, and Stewartstown.

Expansion continued in the early 1960s with the purchase of Plant #2 from the Red Lion Cabinet Company, the Glen Rock facility in Pottsville, and the present-day Red Lion facility at 100 Redco Avenue.

An institutional furniture line for homemaking and arts and crafts was introduced in 1960. Followed by elementary and music lines in 1962. The Library Furniture line was introduced in 1965 and "Quality Furniture for Education" became the slogan for the institutional line.

Colonial's International style cabinets, selected for the World's Fair House in 1964, combined a carefree Formica surface and satin-finish stainless steel to produce an exciting new concept in kitchen cabinet design.

The firm's innovation continued in 1965 with introduction of the new United brand, featuring removable panels made of laminated plastic and/or wood grains with decorator colors. United All-Steel Kitchens soon became a national favorite for builders and architects.

Colonial Products was sold to the Wickes Corporation in 1970 and Charles became chairman of the board. His son, Stephen, was appointed president and chief executive officer. At the time of the sale, the company owned and operated nine manufacturing facilities with more than twelve hundred employees. A year later, construction began on a fifty-thousand-square-foot dimension mill in Mifflinburg, designed to furnish complete wood cabinet parts to all plants.

A new product, Yorktowne Kitchens, was introduced at the National Association of Home Builders (NAHB) show in Houston, Texas, in 1972. Innovations continued throughout the 1970s with laminated plastic door and drawer fronts developed for Yorktowne Institutional Cabinetry and introduction of the TRIO line. The TRIO line was comprised of three solid oak door styles available on a common box. The

✧

Below: Yorktowne's Natural Birch finish cabinets were an innovation in 1951.

Bottom: Spacemaker cabinets by Yorktowne were introduced in 1978 and offered more storage space.

product also featured easy door changes utilizing a snap-in hinge that dramatically reduced distributor's requirements.

In 1980, Connect-ables was introduced as "the cabinet-in-a-carton you put together in minutes." A unique connecting devise held the components together securely. A high-end line named the Signature Series was introduced in 1982 and was marketed as, "Cabinetry so special we even put your name on it." Customers were offered a special brass plaque with their name engraved on it.

By the mid-1980s, Yorktowne operated three manufacturing facilities in central Pennsylvania and an assembly facility in Riverside, California. Yorktowne's products were now sold coast-to-cost in addition to an international market.

Wickes Corporation sold Yorktowne to Berkley International, a financial holding company, in 1988. Yorktowne was then acquired in 1993 by Elkay Manufacturing Company, the world's largest manufacturer of stainless steel sinks and water coolers.

Significant upgrades to Yorktowne's manufacturing operations were completed under the new owners. A continuous flow manufactured program was installed, the drying kilns were rebuilt, and the "Wonder Saw" operation became fully operational. A fully integrated manufacturer of fine cabinetry, Yorktowne starts with green lumber and takes it all the way through to the finished product. By controlling all phases of the manufacturing process, Yorktowne ensures the production of finely crafted, quality cabinets each step of the way.

By the late 1990s, Yorktowne began a shift into the semi-custom field with carefully designed new products including an all-wood cabinet called Platinum. In 2005 the brand introduced the largest product launch in company history. The launch included six new door styles, new finishes, decorative hardware, and a host of new SKU's in every category. A new appliance panel program and custom quote program were introduced to offer kitchen designers additional customization and creativity.

With continued growth and expansion, Yorktowne opened a new "Cane Creek" manufacturing facility in Danville, Virginia. On April 5, 2006, the doors were opened and the plant shipped its first cabinets on March

14, 2006. Through a series of major capital expenditures over a period of five years, Yorktowne is positioned to ensure its high-end semi-custom cabinetry is manufactured in one of America's most technologically advanced operations.

Today, Yorktowne Cabinetry continues its success in the ever-changing world of furniture trends and styles. Now part of the Elkay Cabinet Division, it is the fourth largest cabinet group in North America. Comprised of Yorktowne Cabinetry, Medallion Cabinetry, Schuler Cabinetry and Mastercraft Cabinets, this group has continued to see dramatic growth over the last several years and continues their commitment to improving operations and customer relations within each brand.

❖

Above: Yorktowne's Master Closet Collection, the first in semi-custom cabinetry made for dressing room space.

Below: Yorktowne's Belmont door style in Cherry features our new Merlot finish with an island accented in Onyx.

WOODLOCH RESORT

Woodloch Resort, celebrating fifty years of excellence in hospitality, is nestled in the pristine northeast Pocono Mountains lake region. A resort for all ages and all seasons.

Located along the shores of the beautiful, spring-fed Lake Teedyuskung, Woodloch offers the perfect getaway for an evening, a weekend, a vacation, or a lifetime.

Owned and operated by the Kiesendahl family since 1958, the management team of Woodloch has instilled in the staff the importance of hospitality. Woodloch's reputation for superb service, fabulous food and top-notch entertainment keeps guests returning year after year.

The modern history of Woodloch dates from 1918 when Louise and George Lochwood changed their last name around and christened their estate Woodloch Pines. Three men tended the grounds, which included lawns, gardens, fishponds, fountains and stables. In those days the only way to get to the country was by horse and buggy.

In 1946, a Scandinavian couple, Olga and George Svenningsen, bought the Lochwood estate and turned it into a summer boarding house. Catering primarily to Scandinavians, they hosted about thirty people for "fun and relaxation in an atmosphere of hominess and comfort."

The Svenningsens operated the property for twelve years, but by 1958 the upkeep had become too much for the elderly couple. They reluctantly decided to sell the property and placed an ad in the *New York Times*.

Fate must have intervened on that day because Harry Kiesendahl saw the advertisement in the *New York Times*. He and Mary had vacationed on Lake Teedyuskung as teenagers and were immediately taken by the charm and natural beauty of the property.

By the time Harry responded to the newspaper ad, several potential buyers had already been turned down. But, instead of a fast profit, the owners were determined to sell to someone who would love the property as they had.

After being convinced that Harry and Mary would be the right kind of people to operate the resort, the Svenningsens sold the property for $45,000. The original purchase of 12 acres included 200 feet of lake frontage, the main lodge, annex and two cottages, all of which accommodated about 40 guests.

From those humble beginnings, Woodloch Resort has grown to set new standards of excellence for golfing and recreational communities also.

In 1981, ownership transferred to the next generation of Kiesendahls, with John at the helm as CEO and brother Steven as Executive Director of Sales & Marketing. John's three sons have also followed in the family tradition with Robert, food and beverage director; Matt, director of Woodloch Springs; and Brad, director of rooms and recreation. While John's youngest son Patrick is finishing his education in hospitality, he spends summers and holidays working at Woodloch in various areas, as do other family members. And, as the third generation is groomed to carry on Woodloch's tradition of excellence, the fourth

generation is waiting in the wings.

Woodloch has been recognized by *Family Circle Magazine* as "One of the World's Best All-Inclusive Resorts." Woodloch was also named three times by *Better Homes and Gardens* as one of the top family resorts in the country, and was the winner of the 1999 Pennsylvania "Spirit of Hospitality" Award. The resort has also been deemed by *Parent Magazine* as "One of America's Favorite Family Vacation Resorts" and was named the number one Best Place to Work in Pennsylvania.

Recreational facilities available at Woodloch include a championship golf course, indoor/outdoor pools and sports complex, tennis courts, rifle range, bumper cars/boats, basketball courts, gymnasium, game rooms, batting cages, miniature golf, paddle boats, kayaks and sail boats, waterslide, shuffleboard and bocce ball. Woodloch also offers a wide array of organized games and contests for all types and ages.

Woodloch offers 166 guest rooms and fifty-eight guest rental homes located on more than 1,000 acres. All American Plan vacation packages include meals, accommodations, activities and nightly entertainment.

Woodloch's spectacular eighteen-hole championship par-seventy-two golf course winds its challenging way over 6,579 yards of fern-carpeted forests, lush wetlands and broad upland meadows. With four sets of tees on each hole, all levels of play can be accommodated. The outstanding fourteenth hole requires a 220-yard carry over dramatic 'Hell's Gate Gorge,' which is carved from the rugged mountainside by rushing water some 200 feet below.

The Woodloch Springs golf course has been given national recognition by both *GOLF Magazine* and *Golf Digest* as one of the finest courses in America and has been noted as a 'Rare Find' in *Met Golf* magazine.

In addition to golf and family-friendly vacation recognition, Woodloch Resort is an excellent location for corporate meetings, scout groups, reunions and weddings. Woodloch will help you plan and organize your event from beginning to end with the help of a dedicated coordinator. Woodloch's corporate teambuilding program includes innovative offerings such as Olympic games, scavenger hunts, boat building, health and wellness, and drum circles.

Guests at Woodloch also have privileged access to spa treatments and services, as well as half-day and full-day spa programs just two miles away. Located on seventy wooded acres, the Lodge at Woodloch is dedicated to offering the most advanced spa programming in an elegant lodge environment.

Woodloch is proud of the many fourth- and fifth-generation guests who visit the resort each year. It is the Kiesendahl family work ethic and enthusiasm—reinforced by their loyal staff—which makes each stay totally delightful. Experience the "Tradition of Excellence" that makes Woodloch the ultimate travel destination.

Additional information on this beautiful resort may be found on the Internet at www.woodloch.com.

PCI INSURANCE, INC.

✧

Above: Douglas C. Dyer (left), president and CEO of PCI Insurance, Inc., and Insurance Coalition, Inc., and Floyd Warner, president of the Pennsylvania Chamber of Business and Industry, blazing the trail of employee benefits industry excellence for PCI Insurance, Inc., and Insurance Coalition, Inc.

Below: With more than 150 combined years of service, the PCI Insurance account executives provide platinum consultative services and custom design employee benefit programs for business owners throughout Pennsylvania.

Since its establishment as the Pennsylvania State Chamber of Commerce in 1916, the Pennsylvania Chamber of Business and Industry has served as the frontline advocate for advancing the growth and prosperity of Pennsylvania business.

In the early 1990s, the Pennsylvania Chamber recognized the need to establish an insurance subsidiary based on the overwhelming needs of the smaller businesses in the state to access affordable healthcare. PCI Insurance, Inc., a wholly owned subsidiary incorporated in 1996, offers many of the same healthcare plan and service options available only to Fortune 500 companies.

The program, originally operating in twenty-one counties in Central and South-central Pennsylvania, was well received and grew quickly to become the most popular small group employee benefit plan available in the area.

From 1997 to 2006, the program grew from 20,000 to nearly 50,000 people covered by unique employee benefit healthcare and specialty products. Today, the ChamberAdvantage Program includes more than 5,000 companies and has enrolled more than 100,000 benefit combinations of health, dental, vision, life and disability coverage.

The PCI Insurance Benefit Solutions provide the same features and benefits to small businesses that much larger groups enjoy. The plan treats all participants as one group, giving each participating employer simplified program administration, coupled with the flexibility of choice from a complete portfolio of benefits. Included are multiple Highmark Blue Shield health plans, dental, vision, life, and long- and short-term disability options.

In 2002, PCI Insurance, Inc., became a licensed third party administrator in Pennsylvania to provide a comprehensive "one bill, one HR resource" administrative solution that complemented an already unique product portfolio.

Administering the PCI Insurance benefit program is quick and easy, providing members access to the secure Benefit Administration section of the organization's website. This provides members the ability to administer and manage membership information at one place, saving the small business owner time and money.

PCI Administrative Services include Health Retirement Accounts, Health Savings Accounts, COBRA administration assistance, and Section 125 programs.

Building on its past success and a dynamic strategic business plan, the Pennsylvania Chamber of Business and Industry is committed to positioning PCI Insurance to be the premier employee benefit solution for the small business market in Pennsylvania.

To further strengthen the foundation laid by PCI Insurance with the ChamberAdvantage Program, the Chamber has announced the formation of a sister company, Insurance Coalition, Inc., a full brokerage agency. This adds an even greater selection of employee benefits products and human resource service options for employees of all sizes across the entire State of Pennsylvania.

For more than ninety years, the Pennsylvania Chamber of Business and Industry has taken bold action on behalf of its members. From working closely with the state for unemployment relief during the Great Depression to today's Agenda for Jobs campaign, the Chamber has consistently sought to enhance the expansion of commerce in Pennsylvania.

CROSSETT, INC.

Crossett, Inc. provides transportation services for suppliers and refiners by delivering petroleum-based products to refineries, gas stations, and plants.

The company was founded in 1928 by William F. Crossett, who worked with his father in their small lubricant manufacturing plant on the outskirts of Warren. To deliver the lubricants, Crossett purchased a 780 gallon tank, which he attached to a Model T Ford truck chassis.

Meanwhile, the high cost of rail delivery had caused the National Forge and Ordinance Company to look for more economical means of transportation and the firm approached Crossett about using his unique tank wagon. Seizing the opportunity, Crossett agreed to haul the oil and, with his one truck and one driver, he went into the trucking business.

The company grew and, in 1934, was incorporated as William F. Crossett, Inc. (later shortened to Crossett, Inc.) The second truck purchased by the company had a 1,760 gallon tank, which was one of the very first of its kind. This was just the beginning of Crossett's involvement in innovation and testing of petroleum delivery designs, including the first "double conical elliptical" tank trailer.

Today, Crossett, Inc., is a major petroleum carrier in Pennsylvania, New York, Ohio, and the surrounding region. Company terminals are located in Bradford, Oil City, and Warren, Pennsylvania, and also in Kennedy, Rochester and Tonawanda, New York. Crossett transports millions of gallons of petroleum products annually for customers with the utmost attention to safety and quality service.

The company operates a fleet of 65 tractors, 15 leased owner-operator units, and 183 specialized trailers. The maintenance shop in Warren provides service and repairs for company owned units as well as outside customers' tractor/trailer units. Crossett has an average workforce of 140 employees.

After William Crossett, ownership of the company passed to Robert "Bud" Holder, and then to R. William Holder. Crossett is currently owned by partners President Janet Gregory and Chief Executive Officer Alex Keddie.

The goal of Crossett, Inc. is to provide service to its customers beyond their expectations. Crossett believes the best way to accomplish this is to remain a humble company with "old-fashioned" values such as treating employees and customers in a fair and equitable manner. "We feel the more employees are involved in the business, the more successful we are as a company," says Gregory. "We have a unique culture where business teams, made up of employees from all departments and terminals, meet with management on a regular basis to exchange ideas and implement business plans. We are in a constantly changing industry, therefore every day we are adapting and changing along with it."

✧

Above: Part of the Crossett, Inc. fleet in the 1940s.

Below: A Crossett, Inc. tractor/trailer unit preparing for delivery at a customer's delivery site.

GEISINGER HEALTH SYSTEM

❖

Top: Cardiac Rehab Nurse Susan McTavich, RN, with patient, Joseph Elko.

Below: The Richard and Marion Pearsall Heart Hospital at Geisinger Wyoming Valley, near Wilkes-Barre, Pennsylvania.

From a modest beginning in the small, rural Pennsylvania town of Danville in the early 1900s, today's Geisinger Health System is a sophisticated integrated, physician-led delivery network of hospitals, physicians, outreach clinics, rehabilitation services and insurance services.

The System, which serves a 25,000-square-mile region throughout North Central and Northeastern Pennsylvania, includes a tertiary/quaternary hospital: Geisinger Medical Center in Danville, with the nation's first rural Children's Hospital; a secondary acute care and tertiary hospital, Geisinger Wyoming Valley in Plains Township near Wilkes-Barre; a community hospital, Geisinger South Wilkes-Barre in Wilkes-Barre City; adult and pediatric trauma centers; a nationally acclaimed alcohol and chemical dependency treatment center, Marworth in Waverly, near Scranton; a Heart Institute; Cancer Institute; Neurosciences Program; The Center for Health Research; a national resource for scholarship, advocacy and research; The Weis Research Center; a network of Community Practice Physician Offices; Diversified and Community Health Services; and Geisinger Health Plan, one of the largest not-for-profit rural health maintenance organizations in the country.

Geisinger has achieved national acclaim with numerous listings in the *Best Doctors in America, Best Hospitals in America and Best Health Maintenance Organizations*, as well as in the "100 Top Hospitals"® National Benchmarks for Success Study by *Solucient*.

And it all started in 1915 with Abigail Geisinger. The heiress of a coal mining fortune had an extraordinary vision. She wanted to build a modern hospital in memory of her husband, George. At the age of eighty-five years, Mrs. Geisinger issued a solitary charge, "Make my hospital right. Make it the best." That charge continues today throughout Geisinger Health System.

With nearly a century of experience and growth in more than 40 of Pennsylvania's 67 counties, Geisinger is one of the state's largest healthcare providers and has earned a national reputation for quality, "big-city" healthcare in Pennsylvania's varied and wide-ranging geography.

Geisinger is also one of the region's largest and most important employers. Its approximately 11,000 employees (including more than 650 physicians) contribute to the region's economic and social fabric. Their buying power, combined with Geisinger's investments in people and facilities, results in approximately $3.3 billion annual positive impact on Pennsylvania's economy.

The Geisinger mission is straightforward: Enhancing the quality of life through an integrated health service organization based on a balanced program of patient care, education, research and community service. Geisinger strives to uphold its mission with uniformly high standards throughout its entire health system. Geisinger's motto—Heal. Teach. Discover. Serve—and vision—Geisinger Quality…Striving for Perfection—capture the organization's uniquely focused commitment to the patient and moving healthcare forward in North Central and Northeastern Pennsylvania.

For more information on Geisinger Health System, visit them on the Internet at www.geisinger.org.

Walter Long Manufacturing began in 1898 as a boiler repair shop on Pittsburgh's Southside, but the company story really dates from 1887 when twenty-two-year old Walter Long immigrated to America from England. Life was hard for a working class family in late nineteenth century England and Walter was searching for opportunities not available to him in his native country.

Walter had hoped to find a boiler shop job in western Pennsylvania but after learning such jobs were not available he spent several years working in Cleveland, Chicago, Buffalo and New York. He decided to settle in Pittsburgh because the industrial landscape reminded him of England. A short time later, Walter's brothers, Albert and William, decided to join him in Pittsburgh.

In 1898, Walter and Albert pooled their resources and opened a boiler repair shop on the Southside. The new company also employed their brother William.

The boiler repair shop was actually a rented room on Sixteenth Street where the men kept their tools. The men worked hard and the business had grown into a manufacturing concern by 1902 when the company moved to Nineteenth Street.

Walter Long purchased his brother Albert's share of the business in 1903, although Albert remained as a company foreman until his retirement. More space was needed as the business continued to prosper and the company moved to Muriel Street in 1907.

Walter married Amy Gibson of McKees Rocks, Pennsylvania in 1893 and they had three children, two girls and a boy. The boy, Walter F. Long, was helping around the shop by 1911 and driving a chain-driven Reo truck for the company in 1917, the same year the company bought its first welding machine.

Walter F. Long became president of the company in 1935 and held the position until 1970. His two sons entered the business in the early 1950s, with Walter F., Jr. handling production and Robert taking on sales and

financial responsibilities. Now in its fourth generation of family operation, the Long family tradition of quality and service continues with President Robert I. Long and sons, David S. and Robert G.

An expansion plant in Finleyville, opened in 1972, provided much needed space for administration and larger manufacturing capabilities and is now the company's headquarters.

What began over a century ago as a boiler repair shop is now a modern fabrication company with expertise in bending, roll forming, and welding carbon steel, stainless steel, and aluminum for customers in a wide range of industries. The success of Walter Long Manufacturing is attributed to a dedicated, hardworking group of people who know how to satisfy customer requirements.

WALTER LONG MANUFACTURING COMPANY, INC.

❖

Above: Company founder Walter Long (far right) is shown outside the Southside shop with a riveted tank being trucked to American Tin & Sheet Plate Company in 1922. Standing near the truck is Walter's brother, Albert.

Below: The company's Reo chain-driven truck transporting a tuyere ring to Mackintosh-Hemphill Company in 1928. Tuyere rings, also know as wind boxes, were installed in the base of steel-making blast furnaces.

JUST BORN, INC.

Few products have achieved the iconic status of Peeps®, the yellow, chick-shaped marshmallow confection beloved by children and adults alike. But, as popular as Peeps® has become, it is only one of the many delicious products produced by Just Born, an eighty-five year-old, family-owned confectionery company based in Bethlehem, Pennsylvania.

The Just Born candy tradition actually began in 1910 when Sam Born emigrated to the U.S. from Russia. A candy maker by trade, Born used innovative technology to produce chocolate sprinkles, known as Jimmies, and the hard chocolate coating for ice cream bars. In 1916, Born invented a machine that mechanically inserted sticks into lollipops.

In 1923, Born opened a small candy-making and retail store in Brooklyn, New York. He marketed the freshness of his line of daily-made candy with a sign that declared, "Just Born." Not long after opening the Brooklyn store, Born invited his brothers-in-law, Irv and Jack Shaffer, to join him in the business.

The company thrived in spite of the economic depression of the 1930s and, in 1932, the company moved its operations to an empty printing factory in Bethlehem.

The company continued to grow, aided by several key acquisitions. In 1935, Just Born acquired the prestigious Maillard Corporation, well known for elegant hand-decorated chocolates, crystallized fruits, Venetian mints, jellies and "the best bridge mix in the country."

In 1953, Just Born acquired the Rodda Candy Company of Lancaster. Although Rodda was best known for its jelly beans, it also made a small line of marshmallow products that included a popular Easter Peep that was made by laboriously hand-squeezing marshmallow through pastry tubes.

Sam Born's son, Bob, who had joined the company in 1946, helped mechanize the

marshmallow forming process and Just Born has become the world's largest manufacturer of novelty marshmallow treats, producing more than 4.2 million Peeps® brand marshmallow candy each day.

Other popular products have been introduced over the years; including Mike and Ike® fruit-flavored chewy candies in 1940, spicy, cinnamon-flavored Hot Tamales® in 1950, TeeneeBeanee® gourmet jelly beans in 1977, and sour Zours® in 1999.

Under the current leadership of co-CEO's Ross Born and David Shaffer, Just Born acquired Goldenberg Candy Company, best known for PEANUT CHEWS® and CHEW-ETS®, in 2003. Today, Just Born products are exported to more than fifty markets and the candy is available to more than 1.5 billion people worldwide.

With nearly 500 employees in Bethlehem—plus another 40 at a manufacturing facility in Philadelphia—Just Born is one of the city's largest employers. The company is a strong supporter of community activities, making monetary contributions to local nonprofit and charitable organizations and donating candy to numerous schools, service organizations and public events. Employees are encouraged to help carry out the company vision and philosophy by participating in volunteer activities.

❖

Above: Mike and Ike® packaging.

Below: Just Born, Inc., corporate headquarters in Bethleham, Pennsylvania.

Located on sixteen acres at the edge of Camp Hill and Harrisburg, the Radisson Penn Harris Hotel & Convention Center offers warm hospitality, an inviting atmosphere and superior amenities for both business and leisure travelers.

The hotel began in downtown Harrisburg and the current building was constructed in 1964 when it became part of the Radisson franchise. A recent extensive renovation upgraded and modernized the entire facility, from the meeting rooms to the sleeping rooms, even the hallways and public areas.

The Radisson Penn Harris Hotel boasts a 15,000 square foot Grand Ballroom that is the largest of its kind in Harrisburg. The oval-shaped ballroom, designed as a regal backdrop for community galas, has eighteen-foot ceilings and no pillars. The ballroom is one of sixteen meeting rooms available for trade shows, business meetings and social occasions.

For the last few years, the Radisson Penn Harris, located only two miles from the State Capitol, has been the host hotel for the Governor's Breakfast sponsored by the Harrisburg Chamber of Commerce, as well as the West Shore Chamber of Commerce's Business and Industry Night, which attracts 1,500 people to the Convention Center. The hotel also holds two fundraisers each year, a trade show and silent auction and the Parade of Trees.

As a result of the recent renovation, most of the hotel's sleeping rooms offer Sleep Number® beds, which allow guests to choose the mattress firmness they prefer simply by selecting a number. The spacious rooms and suites at the Radisson Penn Harris feature such amenities as dual phone lines, data ports, complimentary high-speed Internet access, coffeemakers, hairdryers and irons and ironing boards.

Delicious American cuisine served in a casual atmosphere is featured in Bridges Café, open for breakfast, lunch and dinner. Guests of the Radisson Penn Harris may enjoy their favorite beverages during a daily happy hour at Bridges Lounge.

When it is time to relax, guests can enjoy an outdoor swimming pool and fitness center.

Frequent visitors to the hotel or Convention Center may participate in Radisson's Gold Points program. Points may be redeemed for free hotel nights, airline miles, prepaid cards and more.

The Radisson Penn Harris has received the Radisson's prestigious Presidential Award for several years. This award is presented worldwide to hotels that provide high standards of customer service. During annual, unannounced visits, inspectors check for cleanliness and the staff's ability to follow Radisson standards and policies.

The Radisson Penn Harris Hotel & Convention Center is located at 1150 Camp Hill Bypass in Camp Hill, Pennsylvania. For more information, check the hotel's website at www.radisson.com/camphillpa.

RADISSON PENN HARRIS HOTEL & CONVENTION CENTER

✧

Below: Grand Ballroom.

Bottom: Sleep Number® Bears.

RIGHT MANAGEMENT

Right Management Consultants, Inc, was founded by Frank P. Louchheim with the help of three of his associates on December 6, 1980 with headquarters in Philadelphia. The founders were: Frank P. Louchheim, Larry A. Evans, Robert A. Fish, and C. Boardman Thompson, III. The first letters of their last names spelled LEFT, and when they were trying to name the company, Louchheim's wife suggested they could not go LEFT but they could go RIGHT! All four had been associated with the career transition consulting business at another firm, and decided to form a new, national organization. One of their early clients was when Pan American World Airways wanted to downsize in thirteen cities.

They initially had offices in Philadelphia, New York City, and Stamford, and had to quickly add ten more U.S offices, which they did through franchise agreements and by training consultants in the consulting process they had developed. The company was profitable every year, including its first year in business, and went public in November 1986. The firm opened its first overseas office in London when they had an opportunity to deliver a major outplacement project for British Airways. The company used some of the proceeds of its IPO to begin acquiring businesses in Europe and other areas where they needed a presence.

In the early 1990s, Louchheim brought in a new director—former president and COO of Penn Mutual Life Insurance Company, Richard J. Pinola, and shortly thereafter named him as president and CEO. Under Pinola's leadership, company revenues and profits continued to grow and an organizational consulting business was developed to complement the outplacement business. The Company made more than fifty strategic acquisitions in the U.S., Europe and the Asia-Pacific, and purchased back most of these affiliates.

In January 2004, Right Management had an unsolicited bid for its stock from a large company, but decided to seek a different buyer. They then found a "white knight" in the Manpower Organization, and became a wholly owned Manpower subsidiary. At the time Manpower purchased Right Management's stock, the firm had grown to $486 million in revenues.

Right Management has more than 300 offices and 3,000 employees worldwide and is still based in Philadelphia. President and Chief Operating Officer Douglas J. Matthews reports to Owen Sullivan, Right Management's CEO, who operates out of Manpower headquarters in Milwaukee.

Right Management serves virtually all of the Fortune 500, as well as a big part of the Fortune 2000, and many smaller companies, providing consulting services across the full-employment life cycle.

✧

Founder Frank P. Louchheim.

Armstrong World Industries, Inc., headquartered in Lancaster, is a global leader in the design and manufacture of floors, ceilings and cabinets; and the world's largest manufacturer of wood flooring.

Armstrong operates thirty-nine plants in ten countries and has approximately 13,000 employees worldwide. Armstrong's consolidated net sales total about $3.4 billion annually.

This worldwide business began in 1860 when twenty-four-year old Thomas Morton Armstrong bought into the John D. Glass and Company, a small cork cutting shop in Pittsburgh. By 1864, Armstrong was the principal owner.

Armstrong's original business was cutting cork bottle stoppers from bark imported from Portugal, Spain, and northern Africa. Sanitary seals on medicines and beverages were critically important at that time and Armstrong pioneered the concept of brand marketing by stamping "Armstrong" on each cork, as a symbol of quality.

Armstrong also supplied cork dust to linoleum manufacturers who mixed the dust with linseed oil to produce the floor covering. The company, now under the direction of Thomas Armstrong's son, Charles, saw an opportunity to expand and, in 1908, the first Armstrong linoleum was produced at a new plant in Lancaster. By the end of the twentieth century, floor products provided more than half of the company's sales volume.

Under the leadership of Charles, the firm expanded its product lines with cork insulating board, packaging closures, and gaskets, as well as linoleum and related flooring materials.

Armstrong's product line evolved and changed over the decades as it survived the Great Depression, World Wars, and a Chapter 11 bankruptcy forced by asbestos-related lawsuits. The company's core competencies and brands remained solid, however, and today Armstrong World Industries is organized into floor products, building products, and cabinet products.

Armstrong Floor Products is a worldwide leader in the manufacture and marketing of residential and commercial floor products. Its powerhouse family of brands—Armstrong, Bruce® Hardwood Floors, Armstrong™ Hardwood Floorings, Robbins® Fine Hardwood Flooring, and Armstrong Linoleum™—offer the most extensive portfolio of flooring products available including vinyl, laminate, hardwoods, and ceramics.

Armstrong Building Products is a worldwide leader in manufacturing and marketing acoustical ceilings and suspension systems. The business is nearly ninety percent commercial, with two-thirds in improvement projects and the balance in new construction including offices, healthcare, education, retail, and transportation. The residential market, more than ten percent, is primarily in home improvement and remodeling projects.

Armstrong Cabinet Products is a U.S. leader in the manufacture and distribution of fine residential kitchen and bath cabinets and the nation's largest direct distributor of cabinetry. The business received the Environmental Stewardship Program certification from Kitchen Cabinet Manufacturers Association for sound environmental management and sustainable practices.

Armstrong has a history of environmental stewardship. Its flooring business began by using cork waste to manufacture linoleum flooring. Today it fulfills its commitment to environmental sustainability by reducing energy use, seeking and using more renewable resources, expanding its pioneering recycling programs and supporting responsible forest management, among other practices.

The Armstrong Foundation, formed in 1985, contributes millions of dollars to caring efforts in communities where its employees live and work and supports causes employees are passionate about.

For more information about Armstrong World Industries, visit www.armstrong.com on the Internet.

❖

Armstrong World Industries Corporate Headquarters Building 701, Lancaster, Pennsylvania, 2007. This is the first existing building in Pennsylvania to earn the U.S. Green Building Council's highest level of certification.

COURTESY OF ARMSTRONG WORLD INDUSTRIES.

FROCK BROS. TRUCKING, INC.

✧

Above: Quality equipment along with class drivers equates to superior service.

Below: Built on a foundation of superior service, the main headquarters of Frock Bros. Trucking is located in New Oxford, Pennsylvania.

Frock Bros. Trucking, Inc. was established twenty-five years ago with the goal of providing superior customer service, on-time delivery, and quality trucking transportation. Frock Bros. Trucking has grown in both size and reputation since 1982 and has earned its reputation for outstanding service and dependability.

"We treat our customers as we would want to be treated, giving the best possible advantages available when using our services and our fleet," say co-owners Dan and Ed Frock. "We are interested in building long-term relationships by doing everything we can to fill the customer's request. Our customers, both large and small, receive the highest level of competency and customer service from our professional staff of dispatchers, drivers, support personnel, and mechanics. Every representative of Frock Bros. Trucking works to satisfy our customers and maintain a reputation for safe, on-time deliveries and efficient service at competitive rates."

Based in New Oxford, Pennsylvania, Frock Bros. Trucking serves the forty-eight contiguous states and selected Canadian provinces.

Frock Bros. Trucking maintains an enviable on-time delivery record and holds ICC Common and Contract Authority for General Commodities. Vehicles and terminal facilities are continually updated to ensure the best service possible and all operations are staffed by professionals dedicated to the efficient handling of each contract load on an individual basis.

Many Frock Bros. drivers have been with the company since it was established. Employee turnover, so prevalent at other companies, is minimal at Frock Bros. Trucking because employees are treated with respect and considered part of the family. In addition, the company provides top-notch equipment that attracts higher caliber drivers who provide superior service. The driver's conscientious attitude reflects the importance the company places on the driver's role.

Frock Bros. professional drivers, both short-run and over-the-road, are experienced in intra- and interstate hauling requirements and know how to make the best use of available road hours through familiarity with the shortest routes, seasonal road construction, and regional load restrictions. The reputation of Frock Bros. Trucking rests on professional people working together to get the job done on time.

Customer satisfaction is the key to Frock Bros. success and the company does everything possible to make sure each customer's experience with the company is successful as well.

"We understand that our customers value quality, we understand that dependability is an important issue, and that our customers need flexible solutions," says President John Frock. "Because customer satisfaction is the basis of all our services, Frock Bros. Trucking delivers even fragile products such as snack food and housewares, refrigerated items or produce, on-time and on budget."

For more information about Frock Bros. Trucking, check the website at www.frockbros.com.

SPONSORS

About the Author

William A. Pencak

William Pencak is Professor of History at the Pennsylvania State University, where he teaches Pennsylvania and early American history. He edited the journal *Pennsylvania History* from 1994 to 2002. His other works include five co-edited volumes, all published by and currently available from Penn State Press; *Pennsylvania: A History of the Commonwealth*, a multi-authored volume of 650 pages with nearly 500 illustrations sponsored by the Pennsylvania Historical and Museum Commission; *Friends and Enemies in Penn's Woods*; *Making and Remaking Pennsylvania's Civil War*; *Beyond Philadelphia: The American Revolution in the Pennsylvania Hinterland*; and *Riot and Revelry in Early America*. His most recent book, *Jews and Gentiles in Early America: 1654-1800*, was published by the University of Michigan Press in 2005. He has also written articles on Benjamin Franklin, the Pennsylvania Episcopal Church during the American Revolution, and French Travellers in Eighteenth-Century Pennsylvania. His current major project is a history of the family of John Jay, the first chief justice of the United States Supreme Court. Born in Brooklyn, New York, in 1951, he received his B.A. and Ph.D. in history from Columbia University, and has held research fellowships at Duke and Princeton Universities and the Huntington Library in San Marino, California. Previously he taught at Tufts University, the University of California at San Diego, and the University of Monterrey in Mexico as a Fulbright Professor.

A poster promoting Pennsylvania, showing children from a religious community, by Katherine Milhous.

Right: Electric Welder. *Olive Harriette Nuhfer, artist. 1937. Pittsburgh. 28" × 20" oil on canvas.*

NO. 12. COURTESY OF THE EDWARD STEIDLE MUSEUM, COLLEGE OF EARTH AND MINERAL SCIENCE, PENN STATE UNIVERSITY.

Opposite: Men were urged to register for the military draft in World War I as a public obligation by the Committee of Public Safety of Pennsylvania, and given the opportunity to enlist at numerous locations in the Philadelphia area alone.

COURTESY OF THE LIBRARY OF CONGRESS.

For more information about the following publications or about publishing your own book, please call
Historical Publishing Network at 800-749-9790 or visit www.lammertinc.com.

Black Gold: The Story of Texas Oil & Gas

Historic Abilene: An Illustrated History

Historic Albuquerque: An Illustrated History

Historic Amarillo: An Illustrated History

Historic Anchorage: An Illustrated History

Historic Austin: An Illustrated History

Historic Baldwin County: A Bicentennial History

Historic Baton Rouge: An Illustrated History

Historic Beaufort County: An Illustrated History

Historic Beaumont: An Illustrated History

Historic Bexar County: An Illustrated History

Historic Birmingham: An Illustrated History

Historic Brazoria County: An Illustrated History

Historic Charlotte:
An Illustrated History of Charlotte and Mecklenburg County

Historic Cheyenne: A History of the Magic City

Historic Comal County: An Illustrated History

Historic Corpus Christi: An Illustrated History

Historic Denton County: An Illustrated History

Historic Edmond: An Illustrated History

Historic El Paso: An Illustrated History

Historic Erie County: An Illustrated History

Historic Fairbanks: An Illustrated History

Historic Gainesville & Hall County: An Illustrated History

Historic Gregg County: An Illustrated History

Historic Hampton Roads: Where America Began

Historic Hancock County: An Illustrated History

Historic Henry County: An Illustrated History

Historic Houston: An Illustrated History

Historic Illinois: An Illustrated History

Historic Kern County:
An Illustrated History of Bakersfield and Kern County

Historic Lafayette:
An Illustrated History of Lafayette & Lafayette Parish

Historic Laredo:
An Illustrated History of Laredo & Webb County

Historic Louisiana: An Illustrated History

Historic Midland: An Illustrated History

Historic Montgomery County:
An Illustrated History of Montgomery County, Texas

Historic Ocala: The Story of Ocala & Marion County

Historic Oklahoma: An Illustrated History

Historic Oklahoma County: An Illustrated History

Historic Omaha:
An Illustrated History of Omaha and Douglas County

Historic Ouachita Parish: An Illustrated History

Historic Paris and Lamar County: An Illustrated History

Historic Pasadena: An Illustrated History

Historic Passaic County: An Illustrated History

Historic Philadelphia: An Illustrated History

Historic Prescott:
An Illustrated History of Prescott & Yavapai County

Historic Richardson: An Illustrated History

Historic Rio Grande Valley: An Illustrated History

Historic Scottsdale: A Life from the Land

Historic Shreveport-Bossier:
An Illustrated History of Shreveport & Bossier City

Historic South Carolina: An Illustrated History

Historic Smith County: An Illustrated History

Historic Texas: An Illustrated History

Historic Victoria: An Illustrated History

Historic Tulsa: An Illustrated History

Historic Williamson County: An Illustrated History

Historic Wilmington & The Lower Cape Fear:
An Illustrated History

Iron, Wood & Water: An Illustrated History of Lake Oswego

Miami's Historic Neighborhoods: A History of Community

Old Orange County Courthouse: A Centennial History

Plano: An Illustrated Chronicle

The New Frontier:
A Contemporary History of Fort Worth & Tarrant County

The San Gabriel Valley: A 21st Century Portrait

The Spirit of Collin County